International Terrorism:
An Annotated Bibliography
and Research Guide

Other Titles in This Series

Terrorism: Theory and Practice, edited by Yonah Alexander, Paul Wilkinson, and David Carlton

Self-Determination: National, Regional, and Global Dimensions, edited by Yonah Alexander and Robert A. Friedlander

Victims of Terrorism, edited by Frank M. Ochberg

Terrorism and Global Security: The Nuclear Threat, Louis René Beres

Terrorism and Hostage Negotiations, Abraham H. Miller

Westview Special Studies in National and International Terrorism

International Terrorism:
An Annotated Bibliography and Research Guide
Augustus R. Norton and Martin H. Greenberg

All aspects of international terrorism are covered in this bibliography of approximately 1,000 entries, of which one-third are annotated. The authors also provide a research guide and recommend a basic acquisitions list for libraries. Designed to serve students, scholars, libraries, and public officials, this is the only extensive annotated bibliography on the subject.

Augustus R. Norton is an area specialist for the Arab world with the Department of Defense; he has also been adjunct assistant professor of political science at the University of Illinois. Martin H. Greenberg is associate professor of political science at the University of Wisconsin, Green Bay, where he has served as director of graduate studies.

International Terrorism:
An Annotated Bibliography and Research Guide

Augustus R. Norton
Martin H. Greenberg

Westview Press / Boulder, Colorado

Westview Special Studies in
National and International Terrorism

Published in 1980 in the United States of America by
     Westview Press, Inc.
     5500 Central Avenue
     Boulder, Colorado 80301
     Frederick A. Praeger, Publisher

Library of Congress Catalog Card Number: 79-27845
ISBN: 0-89158-461-7

Composition for this book was provided by the authors.
Printed and bound in the United States of America.

*To those who have fallen
before the terrorists' onslaught.
Their memory will long survive
their faceless antagonists.*

Contents

International Terrorism:
An Annotated Bibliography
and Research Guide

Introduction

The currency of the subject of this bibliography is so obvious that it is unnecessary to re-
hearse the litany of outrages delineating the subject. Indeed, any of a number of fine works cited
in the pages to follow do a very credible job of
describing and analyzing the various terrorist incidents and campaigns. Instead what we intend in
this brief introduction is to offer a few general
comments on the terror-violence phenomenon and its
literature and our recommendations as to how the
reader may best utilize this book.

I

Whatever its causes and moral status, terror-
ism--and we use the value-laden word quite self-
consciously--seems omnipresent. Terrorism, in one
or another of its variants, is very nearly a global,
and certainly an international phenomenon. Even as
one of the editors traveled in the Middle East in
1979, there were significant incidents of terrorism
in Ankara, Aleppo and Jerusalem (not to mention
bombings in Madrid), and all of the terrorist acts
were within a span of just a few weeks. Yet,
except for the unfortunate few, life went on, for
terrorism does not assault us physically but rather
symbolically. In fact, the symbolic effect of an
act of terror is often displaced, so that it is
felt most severely many miles from the scene of the
violence. For example, while terrorist murders oc-
curred at the Syrian Military Academy in Aleppo in
June 1979, life in that northern Syrian city remain-
ed as relaxed and congenial as ever. Yet far to the
south, in Damascus, the metaphor of "electricity in

the air" was never so apropos as uniformed soldiers and police, as well as guards in mufti, seemed to even outnumber the simple citizen. Terrorism is the theatre of the macabre, and the audience is only incidentally the spectator at the scene.

For most of us, the closest that we come to witnessing an act of terrorism is through the media, and it is through the extraordinary capabilities of the modern media that violence for effect has become a matter of considerable concern. In short, the age-old weapon, terrorism, has through the magic of mass communications become the prototypical media event. It is close to impossible to read a newspaper, visit a bookstore, scan a drugstore magazine rack, or partake of the electronic media without being made aware of the assault of terror-violence upon our moral senses.

As we know, terrorism has not emerged resultant of the discovery of the vacuum tube, the transistor or the jet engine, but these inventions have all contributed to the heightened salience of this ancient tool of the weak. Terrorism has always been available to the disenfranchised and the discontented as a relatively blunt medium of communication between the power-poor and the ostensibly strong. However, in recent years the size of the potential audience has grown by at least six orders of magnitude. Compare for example, the small audience in the heyday of the nihilists and anarchists of the nineteenth century--in many ways the intellectual forebears of the terrorists of today--to the global audience of the late twentieth century.

While the governments and peoples of this planet face any of a number of tendentious problems, many arguably more serious than terrorism, few problems can compete with the capacity of an act of terror to enrapture an audience. Whereas global inflation, energy shortages, and nuclear proliferation are relatively arcane, terrorism tends to fascinate, even entertain an audience that is otherwise all too often apathetic. Few events can compete with the drama of an ongoing act of terror-violence, replete as it is with suspense, danger, and human tragedy.

With all of this said, we should not be surprised that terrorism has been proven to be a most

2

potent publicity tool. However, we should not allow
the intensity of the drama (or the plethora of books
for that matter) to lead us to overestimate the sev-
erity of the problem. Terrorists only <u>seem</u> omnipresent. Terrorists have achieved no strategic
victories, and the scores of victims pale considerably in comparison to the toll of natural disasters,
wars and the conflict of the highway. The point is
not to belittle the problem, but to assert that an
intelligent regimen of defenses can help to insure
that terrorism remains a topic we read about rather
than experience firsthand.

II

The terrorism problem has spawned an incredible
number of books, articles, and documents over a
surprisingly short period of time. In fact, most
of the entries in this bibliography were published
in the last ten years. The bulk of the materials
which are available is amply illustrated by the fact
that the fiction section alone contains 100 selected
entries, and most of these books have been published
since 1973. Given the large number of materials
publicly available on the various aspects of terrorism, we sought to bring together, in one readily
accessible volume, a reasonably comprehensive bibliography which would help to bring some order to
the literature. Our guiding principle has been to
offer a bibliography in a format which would be useful to researcher, student and policymaker alike.
We would like to bring the following features to
our readers' attention.

A. Organization: The bibliography is basically divided into geographic and topical sections.
In general, where a given work transcends regional
boundaries, it is cited in the appropriate topical
section. Thus, a general work on skyjacking will
normally be found in the appropriate subsection of
the "Tactics" section. Whereas a book dealing with
a Middle Eastern skyjacking would normally be found
in the "Middle East" section. In practice the reader is advised to consult the appropriate topical
and regional sections, since the classification of
a given work is not always clear-cut. In addition,
we have generally allowed the geographic origin of
a terrorist group to determine the appropriate geographic section. Thus, a work treating fedayeen ac-

3

tivities in Europe would be found in the "Middle
East" chapter not the "Western Europe" section.

In the case of general works, especially col-
lections, the reader will normally find multiple
listings. The "General Works" section lists the
work in its entirety, and the appropriate topical
or geographic sections cite individual works contained in the collection. Subsidiary works will
contain the author's name, the name of the contribu-
tion, and a cite as follows: in Entry A-2, 110-
117. (Indicating the complete citation may be
found in the second entry in Section A (General
Works) at pages 110-117.

B. Annotations: Many of the cited works are
annotated to indicate the scope of the work, its
significance and any special features. The most
extensive annotations will be found in the "General
Works" section (Section A), since it is our judgment
that this section will be of interest to the larg-
est number of readers. In addition, the "Nuclear
Terrorism" section (Section H) is extensively annotated, again reflecting the anticipated wide appeal
of that section.

Many works are adequately described by their
titles. Thus, in the case of legal materials and
government documents, we decided to generally
forego annotation. Furthermore, peripheral works,
as in the "Related Works" section, or works of general knowledge are not annotated. This is frankly
to preclude a massive, even cumbersome, book.

C. Fiction: We do not believe that social
scientists, historians, lawyers, practitioners, or
officials have any particular oligopoly on insight
or wisdom. Thus, we have included an extensive
bibliography of recent works of fiction in the
field. Many of these works are especially well-
informed and provocative, and may interest not only
the pleasure reader but the student of terrorism as
well. Those concerned with contingency planning
and scenario building may be especially rewarded
by recourse to this section.

D. Appendices: In Appendix 1 the reader finds
a listing of additional resource materials.

Appendix 2 is a recommended acquisitions list

4

intended as a guide for building a library on the subject of terrorism. A core listing of twelve works represents our best judgement as to the foundation of such a library. The expanded list of 30 titles is meant to accommodate those with the means to acquire a more extensive collection. Obviously, since we cite over 1000 works, we do not pretend that our recommended acquisitions list is the last word on the subject. It is only a start.

E. Index: Our author index refers the reader to each respective work by chapter letter and entry number (e.g. Alexander, Yonah, A-2).

Finally, we would like to thank our compatriots at Westview Press for their patience, Jan Ihlenfeldt for typing the manuscript and our wives for their good humor and encouragement and tolerance of the high costs of transcontinental editing. With each other, we share the blame for any errors which may reside between the covers of this book.

Augustus R. Norton   Martin H. Greenberg
Norfolk, Virginia   Green Bay, Wisconsin

Section A
General Works

1. Alexander, Yonah. "Terrorism, the Media and
   the Police." Journal of International Affairs, 32 (Spring/Summer 1978): 101-113.

   Alexander argues that terrorism is violence
for effect and that terrorists seek to exploit
the symbolism of their act through the attention and recognition available via the mass
media. Furthermore, the publicity given to
terror violence incites imitation, "the expor-
tation of violent techniques." He is concerned that the symbiotic relationship between
terrorist and newsman produces the impression
of a sympathetic media and thus encourages
terrorism. He calls for further study of this
problem and provides worthwhile bibliographic
data on the preliminary study of the issue.
Finally, he calls for a solution to the problem
which will not involve surrendering media
prerogatives.

2. Alexander, Yonah, ed. International Terrorism:
   National Regional and Global Perspectives.
   New York: Praeger Publishers, 1976.

   A useful collection of regionally oriented
contributions. For specific entries see: I4,
K14; M3, 40, 114; N14, 19; and O2, 32. A 40-
page bibliography has been provided, but it has
since been superseded by the more current bibliography in Alexander and Finger (1977) see
Entry A4.

3. Alexander, Yonah; Carlton, David; and Wilkinson, Paul. Terrorism: Theory and Practice. Boulder, Colo: Westview Press.

1979.

Includes contributions by a number of specialists treating terrorist movements in general, Northern Ireland, the media and terrorism, hostage negotiations, counter-terror options, the sanctioning of terrorism, and a prospectus on the future of "political substate violence." The contributors are well-known in the field and include Robert A. Friedlander, Abraham Miller, et. al., in addition to the editors.

4. Alexander, Yonah, and Finger, Seymour M., eds.
    Terrorism: Interdisciplinary Perspectives.
    New York: The John Jay Press, 1977.

    Clearly, one of the very best edited works on the subject. Terrorism is treated from historical, political, strategic, legal, communications and psychological perspectives. See individual entries: A43, 74, 126, 129, 132, 152; F11, 49; H41, M4, 98; N18; and S12.

    The work is enhanced by a 50-page bibliography which includes both scholarly and journalistic references. Many of the articles were first presented at a conference sponsored by the Ralph Bunche Institute of the United Nations in June 1976.

5. Alexander, Yonah and Friedlander, Robert.
    Self-Determination: National, Regional,
    and Global Dimensions. Boulder, Colorado:
    Westview Press, 1979.

6. Alexander, Yonah, and Levine, Herbert M.
    "Prepare for the Next Entebbe". Chitty's
    Law Journal, 25 (1977): 240-242.

    The authors see a future of yet more explosions, hijackings and assassinations. Unless the imperative for international cooperation against terrorism is met, the governments and peoples of the world "will be the hostages of global blackmailers forever."

7. Anable, David. "Terrorism: Loose Net Links
    Diverse Groups; No Central Plot." And,
    "Terrorism: How a Handful of Radical

States Keep it in Business." Christian
Science Monitor, 14, 15 March 1977, pp. 18
and 19, and 14 and 15 respectively.

8. Anderson, W. Age of Protest. Pacific Palis-
    ades, Calif. Goodyear Publishing, 1969.

    (unseen)

9. Andics, Hellmut. Rule of Terror: Russia
    Under Lenin and Stalin. NY: Holt, Rine-
    hart & Winston, 1969.

    (unseen)

10. Avery, William P. "Terrorism, Violence, and
    the International Transfer of Conventional
    Armaments." A paper presented at the April
    1978 meeting of the Midwest Political
    Science Association, Chicago, Illinois.

    An attempt to explore the relationship be-
    tween terrorist political violence and the
    international transfer of arms. Among the
    findings of this preliminary study was the
    fact that riots and guerrilla warfare were
    found only marginally important for armament
    decisions, while armed attacks were found to
    be practically the sole type of political vio-
    lence exerting important influence for such
    decisions. The study is less important for
    what it proves, than it is as a suggestion of
    an additional research direction.

11. Barber, Charles T. "Sanctions Against Modern
    Transnational Crimes." Paper presented to
    the Conference on New Directions in Inter-
    national Relations, Teaching and Research,
    Bloomington, Indiana, May 1976.

12. Bassiouni, M. Cherif, ed. International Ter-
    rorism and Political Crimes. Springfield,
    Illinois: Charles C. Thomas, 1975.

    A very important collection of articles,
    drawn almost entirely from the June 1973 Con-
    ference on Terrorism and Political Crimes
    (Siracuse, Italy). Topics include: origins
    and cause of terrorism; national liberation
    wars; hijacking; kidnapping; jurisdiction and

extradition questions; and avenues for international control. See individual entries: A114,
169, 172; C26, 41; F3, 4, 9, 32, 40, 59, 61,
64, 65; G (Kidnapping) 19, 24; I7; M31, 77.

19 appendices are included, providing the
texts of United Nations' documents, draft
codes and protocols, treaties and other documents and chronologies.

13. Beichman, Arnold. "A War Without End." The
American Spectator, 11 (April 1978):
20-23.

After reviewing the phenomena of contemporary terrorism, Beichman concludes with the
suggestion that the terrorist--the "literal
killer of the literal innocent"--be treated
as an enemy agent caught behind the lines, he
should face capital punishment, and he must
know in advance that a "drumhead court-martial"
will follow his capture.

14. _____. "An Angry Fancy: The 'Politics' of
Terror." Lugano Review, 2/1975: 18-24f.

Beichman argues that there is a relationship between the diminishment of the revolutionary ardor of the U.S.S.R. and the P.R.C.
and the obsolense of violent revolution as a
form of social change in industrially advanced
democratic societies. He concludes the "Permanent Revolution" is no longer with us, but
the "Permanent Revolutionaries" (terrorists)
still are. He sees the "main tendency" in
the world as the slaughter of the innocents,
rather than revolution. All of this compound-
ed by the terrorists' frustrations: workers
not heeding the call to revolution and the re-
luctance of left's intellectuals to act. Since
there is no way a democracy--which by nature
assumes an obedient populace--can prevent terrorism, more lives will be lost.

15. Bell, J. Bowyer. A Time of Terror: How Dem-
ocratic Societies Respond to Revolutionary
Violence. New York: Basic Books, Inc.,
Publishers, 1978.

The prolific J. Bowyer Bell has prepared
an intelligent and highly readable work of

journalism (in the flattering sense of the
term). While the book is less than the subtitle suggests in terms of treating the response to terrorism, it does provide extended
discussions of recent terrorism (from 1968-on),
with particularly good chapters on Italy and
Ireland. In addition, a very detailed chronicle of the September 1976 hijacking of a TWA
flight by Croatian terrorists is presented.
A bibliography, with comprehensive commentary,
deserves the reader's attention as well.

16. _____. On Revolt: Strategies of National
      Liberation. Cambridge: Harvard University
      Press, 1976.

    Includes case material from mandatory Pa-
lestine, Gold Coast, Malaya, Kenya, Cyprus, the
contemporary Middle East, Ireland, and South
Arabia. On Revolt is admirably prepared by
any standard for a descriptive work, but its
lack of an appropriate theoretical framework
will leave many scholars unsatisfied.

17. _____. Transnational Terror. Washington,
      D.C. American Enterprise Institute for
      Public Policy Research; and Stanford,
      Calif.: Hoover Institution on War, Revo-
      lution and Peace, 1975.

    This 90-page monograph offers a concise in-
troduction to the problem of terror-violence;
its breadth is far wider than the title "transnational terror" would indicate. It is probably most useful for the concerned layman.
Bell categorizes "terror" (perhaps excessively)
as follows: psychotic, criminal, endemic,
authorized, vigilante, and revolutionary (including organizational, allegiance, functional,
provocation, manipulation and symbolic terrorism). He discusses terrorism as it has appeared in Palestine, Ireland, Venezuela, Argentina,
and among the fedayeen. Bell allows that there
has been ad hoc "transnational" cooperation
between groups, but he does not find assertions
of a global or regional conspiracy convincing,
thus leaving the reader to wonder why the
author chose the title that he did.

18. _____. "Revolutionary Organizations: Spe-

cial Cases and Imperfect Models." In
Entry A33, 78-92.

Espouses a national (vs. cross-national)
perspective for understanding terrorism. An-
alyses of the Provisional IRA, the EOKA and
the Eritrean Liberation Front are offered.

19. _____. "Transnational Terror and World
Order." South Atlantic Quarterly, 74
(Autumn 1975): 404-417.

20. _____. "Contemporary Revolutionary Organizations," in Robert O. Keohane and Joseph
S. Nye, Jr., eds. Transnational Relations
and World Politics. Cambridge: Harvard
University Press, 1973, 153-168.

21. _____. The Myth of the Guerrilla: Revolutionary Theory and Malpractice. New York:
Alfred A. Knopf, 1971.

22. Ben-Dak, Joseph D., ed. The Future of Collective Violence; Societal and International
Perspectives. Lund: Studentlitteratur,
1974.

(unseen)

23. Bennett, James P. and Saaty, Thomas L. Terrorism: Patterns for Negotiations (Three
Case Studies Through Hierarchies and Holar-
chies). The Wharton School, Univ. of
Pennsylvania, August 1977.

24. Beres, Louis R. "Guerrillas, Terrorists, and
Polarity: New Structural Models of World
Politics." The Western Political Quarter-
ly, 27 (December 1974): 624-636.

25. Bienen, Henry. Violence and Social Change: A
Review of Current Literature. Chicago:
University of Chicago Press, 1968.

26. Bocca, Geoffrey. The Secret Army. Englewood
Cliffs, NJ: Prentice-Hall, 1968.

(unseen)

27. Bouthol, Gaston. International Terrorism in

its Historical Depth and Present Dimension, 1968-1975. Washington, D.C.: U.S. Department of State, 1976.

Noteworthy for its discussion of the terrorism psyche.

28. _____. "Definitions of Terrorism." In Entry A33, 50-59.

29. Bowen, D., and Masotti, L.H. Civil Violence: A Theoretical Overview. Cleveland: Case Western Reserve Civil Violence Research Center, 1968.

(unseen)

30. Brewer, Gary D. "Existing in a World of Institutionalized Danger." New Haven, Conn.: School of Organization and Management, Yale University, Technical Report 102, March 1976.

31. Buckley, Alan D., ed. "International Terrorism." Journal of International Affairs, 32 (Spring/Summer 1978).

A collection of articles dealing with terrorism; most of the contributions are conscientiously analytical rather than merely descriptive. Topics range from a typology of terrorism; assassination in Belfast; mass destruction terror; to terrorism, the media and the police.

32. Burton, Anthony M. Urban Terrorism: Theory, Practice and Response. New York: The Free Press, 1975.

Burton's treatment is not as narrow as the title would indicate, nor as probing as the subtitle might hint. He has provided a competent, readable and useful introduction to political terrorism however. The "theorists," from Bakunin to Fanon are surveyed, with nice sections on Debray and Marighella. The whole panoply of terrorist groups is surveyed including the FLN, BOKA, IRA, Irgun, OAS and the Nazis. Information on the government response to terrorism, particularly the British cases, is of value as

12

well. Several useful appendices (in chart form) are provided including a listing of organizations and personalities in Northern Ireland. The author formerly served in the British Army for sixteen years.

33. Carlton, David and Schaerf, eds. International Terrorism and World Security. London: Croom Helm, 1975. New York: The Halstead Press of John Wiley, 1975.

   Just about one-third of this book actually treats terrorism (about 100 pages of some 330), with the remaining sections treating the arms race, European and Middle East security, and peace studies and the study of conflict. The contributions treating terrorism are relatively general in focus, with some exceptions. For individual entries see: A28 and F53.

34. Carr, Edward H. Studies in Revolution. New York: Grosset & Dunlap, 1964.

35. Chaliand, Gerard. Revolution in the Third World: Myths and Prospects. New York: The Viking Press, 1977. (French edition 1976).

36. Clutterbuck, Richard. Guerrillas and Terrorists. London: Faber and Faber Limited, 1977.

37. _____. Living with Terrorism. New Rochelle: Arlington House, 1975.

   Practical advice for the potential individual victim, with an informed discussion of incidents and perpetrators.

38. _____. Protest and the Urban Guerrilla. London: Abelard-Schuman, 1973.

39. Cooper, H.H.A. "Terrorism: The Problem of the Problem of Definition." Chitty's Law Journal, 26 (March 1978): 105-108.

   An excursus on the difficulty of achieving any simple definition of "terrorism."

40. _____. "Whither Now? Terrorism on the

Brink." Chitty's Law Journal, 25, No. 6
(1977): In Entry A54, 269-284.

A commentary written in the shadow of the
Entebbe success. Cooper suggests that there
is a cyclical nature to terrorist activities
and at this point the fortunes of terrorists
are declining (in what he subsequently identifies as a respite only), whereas state terrorism and repression is on the ascendant--be-
coming as it were, an alternative form of
government. Cooper posits that behind successful (non-state) terrorism we find state
support, a questionable conclusion given the
more recent adventures of German and Italian
terrorists. As a final irony, he postulates
that the Entebbe rescue may have taken the
world closer to a terrorist Armageddon, with
the terrorists seeking to meet state power
with mass destructive weapons.

41. _____. "The International Experience with
Terrorism: An Overview." Disorders and
Terrorism. Washington: Entry A220,
419-442.

A competent overview which stresses the
general ineffectiveness of terrorism as a route
to political change (through coercion). For
a terrorist campaign to succeed in accomplish-
ing its strategic goals (rather than the tac-
tical goals of fear or attention), there must
be: "recognizable struggle for self-determination," at least tacit support among the populace, a strong, sustaining ideology, and
outside sponsorship. Cooper also surveys hard
line vs. soft responses, aviation security and
legal responses to terrorism.

42. _____. "Terrorist and the Victim." Vic-
timology, 1 (Summer 1976): 229-239.

43. _____. "Terrorism and the Media." In
Entry A4, 141-156.

Addressing the role of the media in the
terrorism process, Cooper asserts that the
problem is not with straight reporting, but
with the propagandizing of terrorism. He
argues that the media must be content with re-

14

porting the inherent drama of an act of terror, rather than providing additional drama. In short, the media must see itself as part of the problem, and this, Cooper suggests, is a step toward solving the problem.

44. Crozier, Brian, ed. <u>Annual of Power and Con-flict</u>. London: Institute for the Study of Conflict, 1972-1977.

Annual since 1972. A valuable survey of extremist groups throughout the world. Organized by region and by country, this excellent resource is the best book of its kind available

45. Crozier, Brian. <u>The Rebels: A Study of Post-War Insurrections</u>. Boston: Beacon Press, 1960.

While dated in several respects, this book remains a basic source for material on the Algerian FLN, the Cypriot EOKA and the Vietminh. Part IV "Terrorism," discussing terrorism as a "weapon of the weak" deserves a place on any reading list in the field. Crozier sees terrorism as unlikely to succeed unless there is outside support. In the final analysis, he asserts its success or failure will turn not on the intensity of its outrages but on its (in)ability to cause mounting expenditures on the part of the state. "When the question 'Is it worth it?' begins to be asked, the terrorists are winning. When the answer is 'No,' they have won."

46. Demaris, Ovid. <u>Brothers in Blood: The International Terrorist Network</u>. New York: Charles Scribner's Sons, 1977.

Popular treatment flawed by a susceptibility to stereotypical description and rather marked biases especially in the treatment of Palestinian Arab terrorists and the Federal Republic of Germany. Demaris treats international terrorist links, Ireland, mandatory Palestine, modern Israel, the German Red Army Faction and nuclear terrorism.

47. Dobson, Christopher, and Payne, Ronald. <u>The</u>

15

<u>Terrorists: Their Weapons, Leaders, and
Tactics</u>. New York: Facts on File, 1979.

An attractive and well-packaged overview
of terrorism. In addition to the predictable
topics, the book includes: a 40 page "who's
who" by region and country, in which major
groups are given approximately one page of
coverage each; a brief (20 page) chronology
for the decade through June 1979; fourteen
color prints of small arms used by terrorists;
and a very handy index. On the whole, a very
commendable general work, which holds appeal
for the specialist.

48.   . <u>The Carlos Complex: A Study in
Terror</u>. (NY: G.P. Putnam's Sons, 1977).

More wideranging than the title would indicate, this is a competent--if somewhat hyperbo-
lic--journalistic account of international
terrorism. Carlos represents the archtype
international terrorist--purportedly a Soviet
agent--who has had sporadic contacts with other
terrorists, both individuals and groups.

49. Dowling, Joseph A. "Prolegomena to a Psycho-
historical Study of Terrorism." In Entry
A117, 223-230.

Dowling proceeds from a position that the
anarchist-terrorist phenomenon is part of an
endemic impulse to resolve the existential
isolation of man. He touches upon the insights
offered by Freud, Erikson and Lifton as vital
aspects in any attempt to understand the historical phenomenon of terrorism.

50. Eggers, William. <u>Terrorism: The Slaughter of
Innocents</u>. Chatsworth, Calif.: Major
Books, 1975.

(unseen)

51. Elliott, John D. "Transitions of Contemporary
Terrorism." <u>Military Review</u>, May 1977,
3-15.

52.   . "Primer on Terrorism." <u>Military
Review</u>, October 1976.

53. _____. "Writer-Theoreticians of Urban Guer-
     rilla Warfare." Short Essays in Political
     Science, March 1975.

54. Elliott, John D., and Gibson, Leslie K., eds.
     Contemporary Terrorism. Gaitherburg, Mary-
     land: International Association of Chiefs
     of Police, 1978.

         On the whole a useful collection of pre-
     viously published materials, but not without
     significant faults. Unfortunately, several
     areas of concern, in particular nuclear terror-
     ism and terrorist tactics, are incompletely
     treated or not treated at all. By editorial
     design, terrorism in its regional manifesta-
     tions is omitted, thus leaving the reader with
     only a segment of the picture. Of special note
     are contributions by David Fromkin, Ian Smart,
     Andrew Pierre, David Milbank, Brian Jenkins,
     Jay Mallin, Walter Laqueur, and Edward Micko-
     lus. See entries: A7, 40, 66, 91, 94, 117,
     131, 156, 166, 186; H65, 77; R9, 28; G (Kid-
     napping) 5, 21.

55. Fairbairn, G. Revolutionary Guerrilla Warfare:
     The Countryside Version. Harmondsworth,
     England: Penguin Books, Ltd., 1974.

         See last chapter for comparison of rural
     and urban terrorism.

56. Fearey, Robert A. "International Terrorism."
     An address made at Los Angeles on February
     19, 1976, before the Los Angeles World
     Affairs Council of Orange County. Depart-
     ment of State Bulletin, 74: 394-403,
     March 29, 1976.

57. Foreign Policy Association. "International
     Terrorism: 'Do Something!'--But What?"
     In Great Decisions '79. New York: Foreign
     Policy Association, 1977, 74-83.

         Good overview oriented to a discussion
     group format.

58. Forster, A. "Violence on the Fanatical Left
     and Right." The Annals, No. 364 (1966):
     141-148.

59. Friedlander, Robert A. Terrorism: Documents
     of International and Local Control, 2 vols.
     Dobbs Ferry, NY: Oceana Publications, 1979.

     An outstanding and encyclopedic work that
     is an absolute necessity for any serious ref-
     erence collection on terrorism. Includes 150
     pages of commentary, 93 documents, a bibliog-
     raphy and an index. Documents range from the
     League of Nations Council debate on terrorism
     and the assassination of King Alexander (1934);
     to the U.N. General Assembly, Report of the ad
     hoc Committee on the Drafting of an Interna-
     tional Convention Against the Taking of Hos-
     tages (1978).

60. _____. "Coping with Terrorism: What is to
     be Done?" Ohio Northern University Law
     Review, (1978): 432-443.

61. _____. "Sowing the Wind: Rebellion and
     Violence in Theory and Practice." Denver
     Journal of International Law and Policy,
     6 (Spring 1976): 83-93.

     Friedlander argues that terrorism through-
     out the world is getting out of control. If
     not restrained, he notes that the result may
     be a Hobson's choice--"either a global Orwell-
     ian Future, or none at all." He argues that
     the challenge of rebellion and terror-violence
     will necessitate some restrictions in the fun-
     damental freedoms which are taken for granted
     in the liberal democracies. In addition, "the
     hard fact and cold reality is that the main-
     tenance and preservation of international law
     and order can only be achieved through a volun-
     tary reduction of national sovereignty." A
     most thought-provoking article.

62. _____. "Terrorism and Political Violence.
     Do the Ends Justify the Means?" Chitty's
     Law Journal, 24 (September 1976): 240-245.

     Friedlander defines terrorism as "the
     slaughter of the innocent," and he exhorts the
     civilized community to label it for what it is,
     a criminal activity. "To say that randomized
     terror-violence utilized as a politico-legal
     strategy for ostensible revolutionary ends can
     be condoned and even encouraged, simply be-

cause there is no peaceful or legitimate remedy
for redress, is to replace the rule of law
with the ancient credo of might makes right."

63. _____. "The Origins of International Ter-
    rorism: A Micro Legal-Historical Perspec-
    tive." Israel Yearbook on Human Rights, 6
    (1976): 49-61.

    Friedlander argues that despite contempor-
    ary intellectual sentiments to the contrary
    we can be reasonably clear as to the histori-
    cal origins and composition of international
    terrorism. To support his assertion, Fried-
    lander offers an overview of terrorism in
    history, culminating with the outbreak of ter-
    rorist activity and state repression in Man-
    datory Palestine.

64. _____. "Terrorism and Political Violence:
    Some Preliminary Observations." Interna-
    tional Studies Notes, 2 (Summer, 1976):
    1-3.

65. _____. "Terrorism: What Behind One Passive
    Acceptance of Transnational Mugging."
    Barrister, 2 (Summer 1975): 10-13ff.

    Friedlander sees terrorism as "primarily a
    manifestation of rebellion and revolution
    against law-oriented society." He decries
    the lack of involvement of the American Bar
    Association and regional and local law associa-
    tions in the matter of terrorism. Similarly,
    he criticizes the community of nations for
    their inaction and the imposition of an "in-
    ternational double standard" when dealing
    with the question; this inertia flying in the
    face of basic human rights concepts which
    have become a component of "public internation-
    al law" since World War II. Friedlander con-
    cludes by suggesting statutes which would make
    submitting to a kidnapper's ransom demands a
    crime, for to "acquiesce in evil is to con-
    done it."

66. Fromkin, David. "The Strategy of Terrorism."
     Foreign Affairs, 53 (July, 1975): 683-698.

        Traces terrorism from the Reign of Terror
     to the 1970's. Incisive comments on modern
     terrorism are provided, although the anarchist/
     nihilist variety is ignored. Key conclusion
     is that the terrorist succeeds or fails depend-
     ing upon the response of the victim government,
     which must recognize that the act of terror is
     merely a means by which the terrorist seeks to
     force a response.

67. Gaucher, Roland. The Terrorists: From Tsarist
     Russia to Russia to the OAS. London:
     Secker and Warburg, 1968. Translated by
     Paula Spurlin.

        Apparently withdrawn by the publisher due
     to a successful libel suit, this book traces
     terrorism to 19th century anarchism in Russia,
     through German, Rumanian, Irish, and Jewish
     cases. Its treatment of the Algerian war is
     by far the most extensive section in the book.

68. Green, G. Terrorism: Is it Revolutionary?
     New York: (New) Outlook Publications,
     1970.

69. Green, Leslie C. Nature and Control of Inter-
     national Terrorism. Alberta, Canada:
     University of Alberta, 1974.

        Examines cases of hijackings, kidnappings
     and bombings. Proposes U.N. initiatives, crea-
     tion of international criminal courts, and the
     possibility of an international anti-terrorism
     convention as prospective solutions to the
     terrorism problem.

70. Greisman, H.C. "Social Meanings of Terrorism:
     Reification, Violence, and Social Control."
     Contemporary Crises (Amsterdam), 1 (July
     1977): 303-318.

        An argument to either dispense with the
     term "terrorism" or apply it equally to state
     actor and non-state actor alike.

71. Hacker, Frederick J.   Crusaders, Criminals,
       Crazies: Terror and Terrorism in our Time.
       NY: Bantam Books, 1978; Norton, 1977.

       A wordy and somewhat systematic account of
     terrorism by an informed psychiatrist, who dis-
     tinguishes between state terrorism and terror
     by non-state entities while condemning both.
     Hacker's message is that the response to ter-
     rorism must encompass both flexibility and res-
     traint.   He condemns both surrender and "no-
     negotiation" responses although his criticism
     of the latter is far more pronounced than of
     the former.   His professional involvement with
     the Hearst incident and the September 1973 Fed-
     ayeen action in Austria makes his accounts of
     both cases interesting reading.

72. Hardman, J.B.S.   "Terrorism."   Encyclopedia of
       the Social Sciences, 14 (1934):   575-
       580.

73. Hassel, Conrad V.   "Terror: The Crime of the
       Privileged--An Examination and Prognosis."
       Terrorism, 1 (1977):   1-16.

       Apparently inspired by the notion of "fu-
     ture shock" Hassel traces the appeal of terror-
     ism for the young (17-20 years old), middle
     class, college-educated individual to the root-
     lessness and doubt engendered by modern so-
     ciety.   He finds the psychological foundations
     of terrorism in sadism, masochism and necro-
     philia (erotic attraction to dead bodies).   As
     for the noted participation of women, Hassel
     asserts such participation is an aberrant ex-
     tension of the feminist movement and the stri-
     vings it represents.   For the few who become
     terrorists, the frustrations of seeking peace-
     ful change are said to explain the manifesta-
     tion of aggression (terrorism).   In the end, he
     concludes that the ecstasy of the revolution
     becomes the goal, obscuring we suppose any os-
     tensible goal.

74. Horowitz, Irving L.   "Transnational Terrorism,
       Civil Liberties and Social Science."   In

21

Entry A4, 283-297.

Horowitz describes the dangers of terrorism as an undemocratic process that violates
the civil rights of the innocents and bypasses
the due process of law. Correspondingly, he
identifies the danger that counter-terrorism
(sometimes anticipatory) may "decimate the
social and political fabric." He argues the
need to address the consequences of terrorism--
its social impact--as well as to engage in the
study of its micro-effects (e.g., the aggre-
gate casualties wrought by terrorists). Horowitz exhorts social scientists to avoid being
bought, to avoid tailoring research and its
assumptions, to the sponsoring agencies or
groups. Finally, he is concerned that social
change not be stifled at the cost of democracy.
"To prevent social change in the name of democracy is already to have lost the battle."

75.   _____.   "Civil Liberties Dangers in Anti-
       Terrorist Policies." Civil Liberties Re-
       view, March 1977, 25-32.

76.   _____.   "Toward a Qualitative Micropolitics
       of Terror." Delivered at the Conference
       on International Terrorism, U.S. Depart-
       ment of State, March 25-26, 1976.

77.   _____.   "Unicorns and Terrorists." Deliv-
       ered at the Conference on International
       Terrorism, U.S. Department of State, March
       25-26, 1976.

Stresses the need to understand the political system and understand terrorism as a na-
tional--as opposed to international--phenomenon.

78.   _____.   "Political Terrorism and State
       Power." Journal of Political and Military
       Sociology, 1 (Spring 1973): 147-157.

Horowitz urges that careful distinctions be
drawn between "terrorist" groups to avoid the
inappropriate labeling of national liberation
movements. While it is not clear, using his
criteria that a national group, operating in-
tranationally, can ever be classified "terrorists," his argument is nonetheless an important
rejoinder to assertions of "transnational and

22

international terrorist networks." A provocative, though less than faultless profile of a terrorist is also offered.

79. Hutchinson, Marcha Crenshaw. "Transnational Terrorism and World Politics." Jerusalem Journal of International Relations, 1 (Winter 1975): 109-129.

Hutchinson finds that terrorist operations have produced: 1) superficial compliance among third party states and multinational organizations; 2) recognition, whether in the form of praise or denunciation; 3) counter-violence (with Israel as key example); 4) imitation by other minority, political or criminal groups. She is not optimistic about the prospect for international cooperation against terrorists, but instead points to the possibility (now realized) that states will choose the Israeli solution of direct retaliation. Finally, she does not accept the assertion of a formal global terrorist network.

80. _____. "The Concept of Revolutionary Terrorism." Journal of Conflict Resolution, 16 (September 1972): 383-396.

81. Hyams, Edward. Terrorists and Terrorism. NY: St. Martin's Press, Inc., 1974.

Proceeding from a relativistic conception of law and morality, Hyams--who betrays an ecletic, but largely anarchistic personal ideology--provides a rather sympathetic account of terrorism to buttress his argument that terrorism has indeed been an effective instrument of political change. His argument is flawed by an over-emphasis on the terroristic aspects of political struggles (e.g., the role of the Stern Gang in mandatory Palestine) and a number of explicable errors (e.g., he credits the bombing of the King David Hotel to the Stern Gang instead of the Irgun). Nonetheless, much of the book is highly readable and useful. In particular, his treatment of Ievno Azev, the infamous Russian double agent, who shared his services between the Okhrano (secret police) and the Social Revolutionary Party, is well worth consulting.

82. International Institute for Strategic Studies, <u>Civil Violence and the International System</u>, Parts I and II. London: <u>Idem</u>. 1971.

Published in the Adelphi Papers series (number 82 and 83), Part I is subtitled, "The Scope of Civil Violence," and Part II is subtitled, "Violence and International Security."

83. Javits, Senator Jacob K. "International Terrorism: Apathy Exacerbates the Problem." <u>Terrorism</u>, 1 (1978): 111-117.

84. Jenkins, Brian M. "International Terrorism: Trends and Potentialities." <u>Journal of International Affairs</u>, 32 (Spring/Summer 1978): 115-123.

85. Jenkins, Brian M.; Johnson, Janera; and Ron Feldt, D. <u>Numbered Lives: Some Statistical Observations from 77 International Hostage Episodes</u>. Santa Monica, Calif.: Rand Corporation, 1977.

Further evidence that terrorist kidnapping is not a particularly perilous tactic for the perpetrator (e.g., almost 80% chance that kidnap team will escape death and capture and nearly 50% chance that at least some demands will be met.) A chronological, annotated listing of incidents from August 1968 through December 1975 is provided.

86. Jenkins, Brian M. "Upgrading the Fight Against Terrorism." <u>The Washington Post</u>, March 27, 1977.

87. _____.   "Research Note: Rand's Research on Terrorism." <u>Terrorism</u>, 1 (1977) 85-95.

An informative discussion of the Rand Corporation's research on terrorism. Interesting facts include the statement that 40% of the total research on terrorism has dealt with the question: "Will terrorists go nuclear?" Also of note is the fact that Rand is currently investigating acts which are analagous to terrorism (e.g., "well-organized teams of thieves") to determine the range of feasible and likely

24

terrorist threats.

88. Jenkins, Brian M. <u>Combatting International Ter-
     rorism: The Role of Congress</u>. Santa Mon-
     ica, CA: Rand Corporation, 1977.

     Useful for Jenkins' comments on the unila-
     teral measures that may be considered to com-
     bat terrorism (Jenkins finds the possibility
     of successful international initiatives doubt-
     ful). Specific recommendations include: con-
     sidering measures to reduce terrorist mass des-
     truction threats; considering the role of the
     U.S. military in countering terrorism; con-
     sidering the impact of terrorism on arms trans-
     fer policies; and considering the organization
     of government agencies and departments for
     combatting terrorism.

89. _____. "International Terrorism: Trends
     and Potentialities." Santa Monica, CA:
     The Rand Corp., 1977. Also in Entry A203.

     A very extensive (139 pages typescript)
     and well-done overview of international terror-
     ism by one of the leading authorities. Of
     particular value for the identification of new
     potential targets and implements of terror-
     violence. Jenkins identifies liquified natural
     gas facilities for example, as a particularly
     potent potential target. Other sections treat
     surrogate warfare, trends in combatting terror-
     ism, and recent activities of significant ter-
     rorist groups.

90. _____. "Urban Insurgency and Terrorism: An
     Urban Strategy for Guerrillas and Govern-
     ments." Santa Monica, Calif.: The Rand
     Corporation, August, 1976.

91. _____. "International Terrorism: A Balance
     Sheet." <u>Survival</u>, July/August 1975, 158-
     164. See Entry A93.

92. Jenkins, Brian M. and Johnson, Janera. "Inter-
     national Terrorism: A Chronology, 1968-
     1974." Santa Monica: The Rand Corpora-
     tion, R-1597, March 1975.

     Lists 507 incidents (through April 1974)
     which had "clear international repercussions."
     Based on press reports.

93. Jenkins, Brian. International Terrorism: A
     New Mode of Conflict. California Seminar
     on Arms Control and Foreign Policy, Re-
     search Paper no. 48. Los Angeles: Cres-
     cent Publications, January 1975.

         Jenkins notes that not while the actual
     damage wrought by terrorists has been greatly
     exaggerated, they have attracted world-wide
     attention. His analysis is most interesting
     for his speculations concerning terrorism and
     the future. He notes that modern technology,
     e.g., man-portable anti-aircraft weapons, will
     make possible greater destruction by those
     whose grievances, real or imagined, will not
     be easy to satisfy. He also notes the possibi-
     lity of terrorism as an instrument of surro-
     gate warfare. An annotated chronology of inci-
     dents from 1970-1974 is included; however, the
     reader should take care to read the explana-
     tion that accompanies the chronology since a
     number of possible entries are omitted.

94. _____. High Technology Terrorism and Surro-
     gate War: The Impact of New Technology on
     Low-Level Violence. Santa Monica, Califor-
     nia: The Rand Corporation, publication
     P-5339, January 1975.

95. _____. Terrorism Works--Sometimes. Santa
     Monica, California: The Rand Corporation,
     publication P-5217, 1974.

96. _____. Soldiers Versus Gunman: The Chal-
     lenge of the Urban Guerrilla. Santa Moni-
     ca, Calif.: The Rand Corporation, 1974.

         A succinct (10 pp.) paper contrasts the
     modus operandi of the IRA, Tupamaros, and ter-
     rorists in Brazil, Guatamala and Israel, and
     the resultant governmental responses.

97. _____. Should Corporations be Prevented
     From Paying Ransom? Santa Monica, Cali-
     fornia: The Rand Corporation, publication
     P-5291, 1974.

98. _____. Urban Strategy for Guerrillas and
     Governments. Santa Monica, Calif.: Rand
     Corporation, 1972.

A strategy for forestalling and perhaps
avoiding urban terrorism. Applicable to developing countries.

99. _____. "Five Stages of Urban Guerrilla Warfare: The Challenge of the 1970's." Santa
Monica, CA: Rand Corporation, 1971.

Five stages: gaining publicity, buttress-
ing organization, isolating police from the
populace, producing government repression, and
coordination between the emerging mass movements and the organizers.

100. Johnson, Chalmers. "Perspectives on Terrorism."
Berkeley, CA: University of California,
1976.

Discussion of the 1976 Department of State
Conference on International Terrorism. Identifies the following typology of terrorism:
ethnic, nationalistic, ideological, and path-
ological.

101. _____. "Terror." Society, 15 (November/
December 1977): 48-52.

Explains the increase in international terrorism as a reflection of "new targets" suscep-
tible to terrorist attacks, "new technologies"
of weaponry and media capabilities, and "new
toleration" of terrorists through direct and
indirect support by nations. To counter-
terrorism, Johnson urges action by elected as-
semblies in the form of "special powers enacted
'for the duration'" of the war against terrorism.

102. Johnson, P. "Age of Terror." New Statesman,
88 (1974): 763.

103. Kahn, E.J., Jr. "Profiles: How do we Explain
Them?" (A Profile of Richard Lewis Clutterbuck). The New Yorker, June 12, 1978,
37-40ff.

104. Karber, Phillip A. "Urban Terrorism: Baseline
Data and a Conceptual Framework." Social
Science Quarterly (December 1971): 521-
533.

105. Kissinger, Henry A. "Hijacking, Terrorism and War." _Department of State Bulletin_, 73 (September 8, 1975): 360-361.

106. Kossoy, E. _Living with Guerrilla: Guerrilla as a Legal Problem and a Political Fact_. Geneva, Switzerland: Librairie Droz, 1976.

107. Kupperman, Robert H. "Treating the Symptoms of Terrorism: Some Principles of Good Hygiene." _Terrorism_, 1 (1977): 35-49.

   The Chief Scientist of the U.S. Arms Control and Disarmament Agency suggests that as the publicity value of the current levels of terror subsides, terrorists may escalate their threats to keep the public's attention. Kupperman speculates that "mass destruction extortion" may attract criminal elements to its lucrative possibilities.

108. Lambrick, H.T. _The Terrorist_. London: Rowman, 1972.

109. Laqueur, Walter. "Terrorism--A Balance Sheet," _Harpers Magazine_, March and November 1976. Reprinted in: Entry A110, 251-267.

   Laqueur argues that terrorism, which is "no more than a nuisance at present," has been blown out of proportion by those who equate headlines with power. He commends a stiff-backed policy against terrorists and argues that to do otherwise would invite constant tyranny and blackmail by small groups. His argument that terrorism occurs in cycles and that the current cyclic momentum is downward will be challenged by many.

110. Laqueur, Walter, ed. _The Terrorism Reader: A Historical Anthology_. New York: New American Library, 1978.

   A nice reader including selections from antiquity (Aristotle, Cicero, etc.), the 19th century (Bakunin, Most, Kropotkin, etc.), to the present (Paul Wilkinson, Feliks Gross, Hans Josef Horchem, etc.). Unfortunately, many of the selections are only excerpts, rather than complete materials, so the specialist will have to look elsewhere for sources which have not been "tainted" by the hands of an editor.

111. Laqueur, Walter. <u>Terrorism</u>. Boston: Little, Brown and Company, 1977.

A masterful, yet flawed book which surveys terrorism in broad literary and historical sweeps. Laqueur criticizes the synchronic thrust of much of the contemporary work on terrorism, and offers instead the insight that terrorism has been with us for quite some time. He is particularly enamored of the Russian terrorists of the 19th century, in particular the Narodnaya Volya, which one suspects he sees as representative of what a "moral" terrorist group should look like. Juxtasposed to the continuity of contemporary terrorism, he sees several important discontinuities between the old and new terrorist, prominent among such factors is the lack of restraint and discriminateness which characterized modern terrorism. He posits--briefly--a cyclic notion of terrorism in which the phenomenon ebbs and flows from generation to generation. However, this cyclic "theory" is not convincing at this stage, but instead would demand careful analysis and research. In any event, it does appear that Laqueur has been too hasty in interpreting a brief subsidence in terror-violence (which coincided with the writing of his book) as the beginning of a downward trend. While the book is buttressed with an impressive collection of footnotes, the footnote system he employs is erratic and confusing at times. A number of quotes are unreferenced or ambiguously referenced. Furthermore, a number of incidents are mentioned in passing, and while they might impress the reader with the breadth of Laqueur's scholarship, they demand too much of even the well-informed reader (who might, for example, desire at least some explanation of the Chittagon raid in 1930, rather than seeing it mentioned <u>passim</u>.)

112. _____. "Guerrillas and Terrorists." <u>Commentary</u>, October 1974, 40-48.

113. Legum, Colin. "The Rise of Terrorism." <u>Cur-</u>

29

rent, 147 (January 1973): 3-9.

114. Letman, Sloan T. "Some Sociological Aspects
     of Terror Violence in a Colonial Setting."
     In Entry A12, 33-42.

     Letman focuses on the relationship between
colonialism and terrorism as a manifestation of
the alienation of the colonized. He identifies
four types of alienation (economic, political,
cultural and military), which interact and in-
evitably lead to eruptions of violence. He
presents four behavior models: "passing,"
"zombi," "revolutionary violence" (inspired
by Fanon), and isolated terrorism. Fanon's
keen influence is clearest in Letman's assertion that colonial alienation breeds liberating violence.

115. Lineberry, William P., ed. The Struggle Against
     Terrorism. The Reference Shelf Series 49,
     no. 3. New York: The H.W. Wilson Company,
     1977.

     A collection of previously published mater-
ials on terrorism. Includes articles by Fromkin (A66), Hoffacker (R16), et. al.

116. Liston, Robert A. Terrorism. Nashville:
     Thomas Nelson, Inc., Publishers, 1977.

     Terrorism is a diatribe against terrorism
by states, terrorism by revolutionaries, and
terrorism by criminals. Liston tells us very
little about the phenomenon other than the
"fact" that it is almost always unnecessary.
The attentive newspaper reader will find very
little new information in this book, although
a chapter--anecdotal in focus--which treats
efforts to combat terrorism may be marginally
useful.

117. Livingston, Marius H., ed.; with Kress, Lee B.,
     and Wanek, Marie G. International Terror-
     ism in the Contemporary World. Westport,
     Conn.: Greenwood Press, 1978.

     Over 40 papers from the International Sym-
posium on Terrorism held at Glassboro State
College (N.J.) in 1976. Contributors include

Robert A. Fearey, J. Bowyer Bell, Edward Mickolus, Edgar O'Ballance, Brooks McClure, H.H.A.
Cooper, Robert Friedlander, Jay Mallin, R.
William Mengel, Ernest Evans, et. al. Unfortunately, several of the contributions, at
least a third, appeared in print subsequent to
the conference and in more comprehensive form
than they appear in the present volume.
Nonetheless, a number of contributions deserve
the reader's attention and have been cited in-
dividually, see: A49, 188, 239; G (Assass.)
7, H61; J10, 15; K18, M33; O60; R13. An 18 pp.
summary of the symposium, prepared by Marie
Wanek is provided, as is a 30-page bibliography, which was prepared by Lee Kress.

118. McClure, Brooks. The Dynamics of Terrorism.
      Gaithersburg, Md.: International Associa-
      tion of Chiefs of Police, 1976.

      This monograph is intended for a profess-
ional police audience. The scope of the effort
is wide-ranging, including brief discussions
of the variants of terrorism, its origins,
causes, and recruitment patterns. Useful sections treat reactions to terrorism and countermeasures.

119. McGuire, E.P. "The Terrorist and the Corpora-
      tion." Across the Board, 14 (May 1977):
      11-19.

120. McKnight, Gerald. The Terrorist Mind: Why
      They Hijack, Kidnap, Bomb and Kill. Indi-
      anapolis: The Bobbs-Merrill Company, Inc.,
      1974.

      A disappointing book which delivers far
less than the title suggests. Rather than a
systematic treatment of the terrorist mind,
the reader instead encounters a series of interviews, anecdotal in focus, which vary in
their value. The most useful materials concern
the fedayeen, IRA and Latin American terrorists.

121. Mack, A. "Non-Strategy of Urban Guerrilla War-
      fare." In Entry A143, pp. 22-45.

122. Macomber, William B., Jr. "Deputy Under Secre-

tary Macomber Discusses Terrorism in Interview on 'Today' Program." Department of
State Bulletin, 68 (April 2, 1973): 399-
402.

123. Mallin, Jay. "Terrorism as a Military Weapon."
Air University Review, 22 (January/February
1977): 54-64.

Mallin's controversial thesis is that military tactics subsume terrorism. Thus he sees
the Black September attack at the 1972 Olympics
as "fundamentally a military move." Mallin
asserts that "when soldiers fail, terrorists
take over," and yet many terrorists are soldiers. Terrorism is a military tactic when:
it substitutes for regular warfare, when it
is used in conjunction with other military
activities, and when it is used as a chosen
weapon by a population segment against another
segment or foreign power. Terror as a military
weapon can have the following functions: psychological warfare, material destruction, and
economic damage. Problematically, Mallin seems
to blur the distinction between counter-terror
actions by a state and state-terrorism. He
concludes by criticizing the military's lack
of appreciation of the importance of terrorism.

124. _____. "Terrorism in Revolutionary Warfare."
Strategic Review, 2 (Fall 1974): 48-55.

125. Manor, F.S. "Liberal Terror." The American
Spectator, October 1978, 19-21.

In a rejoinder to Merritt (Entry 049),
Manor passionately argues in favor of the res-
trictions that the Federal Republic has put
into force to forestall terrorism. Stripping
away the polemic, Manor's argument is that communism ("of whatever hue") actively seeks the
establishment of a replacement regime which
would "supplant free democracy and abolish human rights," an argument which is ipso facto
justification for the measures instituted in
West Germany. Unfortunately, Manor does not
address the possibility of an overreaction in
a rightward direction, obviously a matter that
deserves equal time (viz. at what point do the
preventive measures themselves become excess-
ive?).

126. Margolin, Joseph. "Psychological Perspectives in Terrorism." In Entry A4, 270-282.

A pithy survey of the possibly fruitful directions that behavioral research into terrorism may travel. Margolin is critical of much of the behaviorally-oriented works to date because of their parochialism ("the unproven assumption that the terrorist is sick"). Included are brief discussions of the frustration-aggression theory, the goal gradient, Ziegarnik effect, uncertainty principle, cognitive style, the study of stimulus deprivation and projected research needs. On a whole a very well-argued piece with significant "hints" for additional research.

127. May, W.F. "Terrorism as Strategy and Ecstasy." Social Research, 41 (Summer 1974): 277-298.

(unseen)

128. Mickolus, Edward F. "Chronology of Transnational Terrorist Attacks Upon American Business People, 1968-1976." Terrorism, 1 (1978): 217-235.

129. _____. "Statistical Approaches to the Study of Terrorism." In Entry A4, 209-269.

A useful compilation from the ITERATE (International Terrorism: Attributes of Terrorist Events) project. Data includes: incidents, by type, 1968-1975; casualties, 1969-1975; location of incidents; nationality of victims and targets; groups, by type of incident and region; as well as supporting bibliographic cites. In addition the ITERATE coding sheet (107 items) is reproduced.

130. _____. Codebook: ITERATE (International Terrorism: Attributes of Terrorist Events). Ann Arbor, Michigan: Inter-University Consortium for Political and Social Research, University of Michigan, 1976.

131. Milbank, David L. Research Study: International and Transnational Terrorism: Diagnosis and Prognosis. Washington, D.C.:

Office of Political Research, Central Intelligence Agency, PR 76 10030, April
1976.

A solid study notable for its prognosis
that "transnational terrorism" (carried out by
autonomous non-state actors) is more likely
to pose an increasing problem for the future
than "international terrorism" (carried out
by terrorists controlled by a sovereign state).
Among Milbank's predictions is the--as yet un-
realized--assertion that transnational terrorism will be more sharply felt in the U.S. in
the years ahead.

132. Miller, James A. "Political Terrorism and Insurgency: An Interrogative Approach."
In Entry A4, 65-87.

133. Milte, K. "Terrorism and International Order."
Australian and New Zealand Journal of
Criminology, 8 (June 1975): 101-111.

(unseen)

134. Milte, K.L.; Bartholomew, A.A.; O'Hearn, D.J.;
and Campbell, A. "Terrorism: Political
and Psychological Considerations." Australian and New Zealand Journal of Criminology, 9 (June 1976): 89-94.

(unseen)

135. Momboisse, Raymond M. Blueprint of Revolution:
The Rebel, The Party, the Technique of Re-
volt. Springfield, Illinois: Charles C.
Thomas, 1970.

Includes useful treatments of terror assassination and urban guerrilla warfare.

136. Moss, Robert. "Urban Guerrilla Warfare." In
Crime and Justice, 1971-1972: An AMS An-
thology. Edited by Jackwell Susman. New
York: AMS Press, Inc., 1974.

(unseen)

137. _____. "International Terrorism and Western
Societies." International Journal XXVIII,

no. 3 (Summer, 1973): 418-430.

Proceeding from the finding that the modern city is singularly vulnerable to terrorists who are increasingly becoming an international phenomenon, finds that the danger for western societies is not that they will be overturned, but rather that they will be provoked into repression measures which will corrode democratic institutions. Moss sees the solution in more effective cooperation among target states, complemented by a heightened concern with the problem.

138. _____. The War for the Cities. New York: Coward, McCann and Geoghagan, 1972.

Although somewhat overtaken by events, this book, by a reknowned British authority, remains a masterful descriptive survey of urban terrorism. Moss's overarching theme is that "terrorism is a faulty weapon that often misfires." Notable sections of the book treat terrorism as exercised in Cyprus, Northern Ireland, Brazil, Venezuela, Guatemala, Uruguay and Tsarist Russia. Discussions of terrorists' ideologies also merit attention. Symptomatic of the analytical problems that plague the literature, Moss's distinction between the "urban guerrilla" and the "terrorist" is less than rigorous and is at times even contradictory to the case examples he provides.

139. _____. "Urban Guerrilla War." Adelphi Papers, No. 79 (1971). London: International Institute for Strategic Studies, 1971.

A terse monograph which neatly summarizes many of the analytical points made by Moss in his The War for the Cities. Marighella's Minimanual of the Urban Guerrilla is appended.

140. Mosse, Hilde L. "The Media and Terrorism." In Entry A117, 282-286.

141. Nasution, Abdul Haris. Fundamentals of Guerrilla Warfare. New York: Praeger, 1965.

(unseen)

142. Neale, William D. "Terror--Oldest Weapon in the Arsenal." Army, August 1973, 10-17.

A workman-like treatment marred by several important errors, in particular the role of terrorism in mandatory Palestine and the support engendered by the Irgun. Neale identifies three variants: vigilante terror, reign of terror (state terrorism) and siege of terror (revolutionary terrorism). He ignores the anarchist/nihilist variant. The treatment suffers from the tendency to call every "terrible" act terrorism, thus we find the Dresden attack and Hiroshima offered as examples because they were terrifying, rather than constituting a program of terrorism (cf. Stalin's terrorism, Hitler's genocide, and the French Reign of Terror).

143. Niezing, J., ed. Urban Guerrilla: Studies on the Theory, Strategy, and Practice of Political Violence in Modern Societies. Rotterdam, Netherlands: Rotterdam University Press, 1974.

A collection of essays which are basically skeptical as to the existence of a "strategy" of urban guerrilla warfare, as well as the utility of this form of violence. Includes materials on U.S., Latin American, and the Dutch Resistance (WW II) movement's activities.

144. O'Brien, Conor Cruise. "On Violence and Terror." Dissent, 24 (Fall 1977): 433-436.

145. _____. "Liberty and Terrorism." International Security, 2, no. 2 (Fall, 1977): 56-67.

O'Brien's distinction between the millenarian and the secessionist/irredentist terrorist is probably worthy of adoption (cf. the loose use of the anarchist/nihilist label).

146. O'Neill, Bard E.; Alberts, D.J.; and Rossetti, Stephen; eds. Political Violence and Insurgency. Arvada, Colorado: Phoenix Press, 1974.

Case studies dealing with insurgents in

Ireland, Thailand, Uruguay, Guatemala, Iraq, and the Portuguese African colonies. The emphasis is upon what has happened, rather than why.

147. Oppenheimer, Martin. The Urban Guerrilla. Chicago: Quadrangle, 1969.

148. Paine, Lauran. Terrorists. London: Robert Hale and Co., 1975.

   Material is included on Palestinian and Canadian terrorists, the Tupamaros, Black Panthers and the IRA.

149. Parry, Albert. Terrorism: From Robespierre to Arafat. New York: Vanguard Press, 1976.

   A polemic against terrorism, particularly in its "leftwing" variants and Marxism. Parry holds the Soviet Union to blame for much of the world's contemporary terrorism. While the breadth of his treatment is farreaching and promising, his lack of detachment limits the scholarly value of the book. Furthermore, there is a very discernible tendency to call all political violence terrorism, which must raise certain questions about the author's understanding of terrorism.

150. Paul, Leslie. The Age of Terror. Boston: The Beacon Press, 1951.

151. Paust, Jordan J. "Responses to Terrorism: A Prologue to Decision Concerning Measures of Sanction." Stanford Journal of International Studies, 12 (1977).

152. _____. "A Definitional Focus." In Entry A4, 18-29.

   An excursus on the problem of defining terrorism. Paust argues for a working definition that would be preferable to confusion resultant of attempts at absolute precision (e.g., in the U.N.).

153. Payne, Robert. The Terrorist: The Story of the Forerunners of Stalin. New York: Funk and Wagnalls, 1957.

154. _____. Zero: Story of Terrorism. New
York: John Day, 1950.

155. Peterson, R.W. International Terrorism Threat
Analysis. Springfield, VA: National Technical Information Service, 1977.

Using the CIA's International Terrorism:
Attributes of Terrorist Events (ITERATE) file,
an attempt is made to identify future threats.
The results were quite inconclusive.

156. Pierre, Andrew J. "The Politics of International Terrorism." Orbis, 19 (Winter
1976): 1251-1269. (Abbreviated version
appears in Survival, May/April 1976, 60-
67.)

Pierre presents an overview of terrorism
in which he identifies six motivations for the
terrorist: gaining political goals, seeking
attention and publicity, eroding or undermining
support for the state, compensating for lack of
political access, liberating colleagues, and
gaining financial rewards. He surveys the recent history of hijacking, kidnapping and U.N.
attempts to seek solution of the problem. He
proposes that counter-efforts combine "prevention" with deterrence. Prevention including
acting on legitimate grievances and rewarding
groups which abstain from terrorism. As to deterrence, he promotes: agreements to the effect that terrorists will be punished for their
acts; international sanctions against those who
harbor terrorists; the sharing of intelligence;
a review of "no ransom policies"; and, the
seeking of a consensus that certain acts are
beyond the pale of legal and moral acceptabi-
lity. Pierre was a Senior Research Fellow with
the Council on Foreign Relations when he wrote
this article.

157. Pfaff, William. "Reflections (Terrorism)."
The New Yorker, September 18, 1978, 135ff.

Discusses the anarchic terrorists of Italy
and Germany and concludes that they more nearly
manifest fascism than any leftist ideology.
Pfaff argues that the terrorists' significance
lies in what they "reveal to us about the deep

preoccupations and anxieties of the national societies in which they act," factors which are resultant of long standing intellectual trends which are only now experienced de novo.

158. Plastrik, S. "On Terrorism." Dissent, 21 (Spring 1974): 143.

159. Price, H. Edward Jr. "The Strategy and Tactics of Revolutionary Terrorism." Comparative Studies in Society and History, 19 (January 1977): 52-66.

A competent review of the literature in which--following Chalmers Johnson--Price suggests that terrorism may be the revolutionary paradigm of the 1970's.

160. Quintero Morente, Frederico. "Terrorism." Military Review, December 1965, 55-57.

161. Rapoport, David C. Assassination and Terrorism. Toronto: Canadian Broadcasting Co., 1971.

First presented by the CBC, this book is an expanded version of the series. Includes historical survey of assassination and its perpetrators, and a treatment of modern terrorism and its antecedents. Nachayev's Revolutionary Catechism is reproduced and a bibliography on assassination (and terrorism) is provided.

162. Reisman, W.M. "Private Armies in a Global War System: Prologue to Decision." Virginia Journal of International Law, 14 (1973).

(unseen)

163. Rothstein, Andrew. "Terrorism--Some Plain Words." Labour Monthly, September 1973, 413-417.

(unseen)

164. Roucek, Joseph S. "Sociological Elements of a Theory of Terror and Violence." American Journal of Economics and Sociology, 21 (Spring 1962): 165-172.

165. Russell, Charles A. "Transnational Terrorism,"

Air University Review, v. XXVII, no. 2
(January-February 1976): 26-35.

166. Russell, Charles A. and Miller, Bowman H. "Profile of a Terrorist." *Military Review*, August 1977, 21-34.

One of the better attempts to profile terrorists. Includes data on age, sex, marital status, rural versus urban origins, socioeconomic background, education, and the method-locale of recruitment.

167. Russell, Charles A.; Banker, Leon J., Jr.; Miller, Bowman. "Out-Inventing the Terrorist." Washington: U.S. Air Force, Office of Special Investigations, 1977. In Entry A203.

A lucid overview which treats terrorist groups, capabilities, motivation and targets, as well as mass disruption terrorism (e.g. operations against transportation or communication networks) and mass destruction terrorism. The authors successfully combine the tools of historical research with speculative analysis. They see the likelihood of terrorism "increasingly becoming an end in itself." "This would result from a nihilist attitude which already appears ...quite prevalent..." They point to the possibility of terrorists attempting disruption operations or even small-scale destruction operations using high-technology or bacteriological resources.

168. Ryter, Stephen L. "Terror: A Psychological Weapon." *The Review*, May-June 1966, 145-150.

(unseen)

169. Salomone, Franco. "Terrorism and the Mass Media." In Entry A12, 43-46.

170. Schreiber, Jan. *The Ultimate Weapon: Terrorists and World Order*. New York: William Morrow and Company, Inc., 1978.

Schreiber's sympathetic treatment of the terrorist fails to seriously challenge prevail-

ing intellectual assessments because the
book is simply too sophomoric. Imprecision,
confusion and error confound this attempt to
prove that denied legitimate access to power,
all men and women are potential terrorists.

171. Segre, D.U., and Adler, J.H. "Ecology of Ter-
         rorism." Encounter, 40 (February 1973):
         17-24.

172. Sewell, Alan F. "Political Crime: A Psycho-
         logist's Perspective." In Entry A12,
         11-26.

173. Shipley, P. Trotskyism: "Entryism" and Per-
         manent Revolution. London: Institute
         for the Study of Conflict, 1977.

174. Shultz, Richard. "Conceptualizing Political
         Terrorism: A Typology." Journal of In-
         ternational Affairs, 32 (Spring/Summer
         1978): 7-15.

     Shultz offers a useful, if not definitive
typology of political terrorism that categorizes terrorism into three basic types--and
then proposes that these types be examined by
variation according to cause, environment,
goals, strategy, means, organization and the
nature of participants. The value of the
proposal is that it offers some hope that
the study of terrorism can move somewhat
beyond the descriptive and journalistic treatments which are currently in vogue.

175. Sim, Richard. "Research Note: Institute for the Study of Conflict." <u>Terrorism</u>, 1 (1978): 211-215.

The activities of the Institute for the Study of Conflict.

176. Singh, Baljit. "Political Terrorism: An Over-view."

A paper presented at the 1976 meeting of the Midwest Political Science Association, Chicago, Illinois.

177. <u>Skeptic, The</u>. "Terrorism." January-February 1976.

A theme issue.

178. Sloan, Stephen. "International Terrorism: Academic Quest, Operational Art and Policy Implications." <u>Journal of International Affairs</u>, 32 (Spring/Summer 1978): 1-5.

179. Sloan, Stephen, and Kearney, Richard, "Non-Territorial Terrorism: An Empirical Approach to Policy Formation." <u>Conflict: An International Journal for Conflict and Policy</u>, 1 (1978): 131-144.

The authors propose that their concept of "non-territorial terrorism" replace the imprecise "international" and "transnational terrorism" terms. But given the common recognition that terrorism takes several forms (e.g. anti-colonial terror, establishment terrorism, "international terrorism"), it is not clear that they have done any more than discover new adjectives. Excepting the definitional attempts, the article offers some interesting conclusions from the study of 111 incidents from 1968-1976, including the fact that most victims have overt political connections (this contrast to the "murder of the innocents" line of argument), and that most terrorists attain legal or pseudo-legal entry into their target territory.

180. Smart, Ian M.H. "The Power of Terror." International Journal, 30 (Spring 1975). Reprinted in Entry A54, 25-33.

181. Smith, Colin. Carlos: Portrait of a Terrorist. New York: Holt, Rinehart and Winston, 1976.

Drawing on interviews and eyewitness accounts, as well as secondary sources, Smith provides a commendable biography of Illich Ramirez Sanchez "Carlos" and the PFLP,(the organization with which Carlos has been most closely identified). The best book available on the subject.

182. Smith, D. "Scenario Reality: A New Brand of Terrorism." Nation, March 30, 1974, 392-394.

183. Sobel, Lester A., ed. Political Terrorism, volume 2: 1974-1978. New York: Facts on File, Inc., 1978.

Through May 1978.

184. _____. Political Terrorism. New York: Facts on File, Inc., 1975.

Drawn from the Facts on File standard library reference, this is a handy compiliation of news accounts through 1974. Indexed.

185. Sterling, Claire. "The Terrorist Network." Atlantic, November 1978, 37-47.

A rather simplistic journalistic account of European terrorism, particularly as practiced by the Red Army Faction and the Red Brigades. Sterling's conclusion that today's urban guerrillas are not unbeatable, raises far more questions than it answers. However, those segments of the article that address state-actor support for terrorists are of some value

(esp. with reference to the Cuban and the War-
saw Treaty Organization countries' relation-
ships with terrorists).

186. Stiles, Dennis W. "Sovereignty and the New
     Violence." Air University Review, 27
     (July-August 1976): 39-95.

187. Stohl, Michael, ed. The Politics of Terror:
     A Reader in Theory and Practice. New York:
     Marcel Dekker, 1977.

     Includes selections by T.R. Gurr (terrorism
     in the 1960's), P.N. Grabosky (urban terrorism),
     H.R. Tary (revolutionary terrorism), E. Mick-
     olus (transnational terrorism), R.R. Corrado
     (European ethnic and student terrorism), M.R.
     Welfling (sub-Sahara Africa), J.W. Sloan
     (Latin America), V.F. Bishop (fedayeen), R.C.
     Hula (Bengal), and F.D. Homer (U.S.).

188. Storr, Anthony. "Sadism and Paranoias." In
     Entry 117, 231-239.

189. Strentz, Thomas. "The Terrorist Organizational
     Profile: A Psychological Evaluation."
     In Entry A202, 757-785.

190. Syrkin, Marie. "Political Terrorism." Mid-
     stream, 18 (1972): 3-11.

191. Tannenbaum, Jeffrey A. "The Terrorists." The
     Wall Street Journal, January 4, 1977.

192. Taylor, D.L. "Terrorism and Criminology: The
     Application of a Perspective. West Lafay-
     ette, Ind.: Purdue University Institute
     for the Study of Social Change, 1978.

     (unseen)

193. Taylor, Edmond. "The Terrorists." Horizon,
     Summer, 1973, 58-65.

194. "Terrorism and Marxism." Monthly Review, 24
     (November 1972): 1-6.

195. Thompson, W. Scott. "Political Violence and
     the 'Correlation of Forces.'" Orbis, 19

(Winter 1976): 1270-1288.

196. Thornton, Thomas P. "Terrorism as a Weapon of
     Political Agitation." In Internal War:
     Problems and Approaches, ed. by Harry Eck-
     stein. New York: The Free Press, 1974.
     71-99.

     The seminal article on the subject. Thorn-
     ton defines terrorism as "...a symbolic act
     designed to influence political behavior by
     extranormal means, entailing the use of threat
     of violence."

197. U.S. Congress. House. Judiciary Committee.
     Internationally Protected Persons Bills:
     Unsworn Declaration Bills, Hearings, June
     30, 1976. 94th Cong., 2nd Sess., 1977.

198. U.S. Congress. House. International Relations
     Committee. Toward Improved U.S.-Cuba Rela-
     tions. Committee Print, May 23, 1977.
     95th Cong., 1st Sess., 1977.

199. U.S. Congress. House. Judiciary Committee.
     FBI Oversight, Part 3, Hearings, February
     11, 1976. 94th Cong., 2nd Sess., 1977.

200. U.S. Congress. House. Judiciary Committee.
     Implementing International Conventions
     Against Terrorism, House Report 94-1614,
     September 18, 1976. 94th Cong., 2nd
     Sess., 1976.

201. U.S. Congress, House. Committee on Foreign Af-
     fairs. International Terrorism, Hearings
     Before the Sub-committee on the Near East
     and South Asia. 93rd Cong., 2nd Sess.,
     June 11-24, 1974.

202. U.S. Congress. Senate. Committee on Govern-
     mental Affairs. An Act to Combat Interna-
     tional Terrorism, Hearings Before the Com-
     mittee, January 23, 25, 27, 30, February
     22; March 22, and 23, 1978. 95th Cong.,
     2nd Sess., 1978.

     Over 1000 pages of hearings, statements
     and appended materials. Included are a number
     of chronologies, reproduced articles and sta-

tistical materials of great value to the researcher.

203. U.S. Congress. Senate. Committee on Governmental Affairs. An Act to Combat International Terrorism, Report of the Committee on S. 2236. 95th Cong., 2nd Sess., 1978.

In addition to the hearing summaries, several important studies are appended, including: B.M. Jenkins, "International Terrorism: Trends and Potentialities:" R.H. Kupperman, "Facing Tomorrow's Terrorist Incidents Today; F.M. Ochberg, "The Victim of Terrorism--Psychiatric Considerations;" and L.A. Russell, L.J. Banker, and B. Miller, "Out-Inventing the Terrorist."

204. U.S. Congress. Senate. Committee on Foreign Relations, Combating International and Domestic Terrorism, Hearings on S. 2236. 95th Cong., 2nd Sess., 1978.

205. U.S. Congress. Senate. Foreign Relations Committee. With Respect to the Release of Abu Daoud, Senate Report 95-1. 95th Cong., 1st Sess., 1977.

206. U.S. Congress. Senate. Commission on the Operation of the Senate. Major U.S. Foreign and Defense Policy Issues. Committee Print. 95th Cong., 1st Sess., 1977.

207. U.S. Congress. Senate. Commerce, Science and Transportation Committee. National Tourism Policy Study, Hearings, April 5, 1976. 94th Cong., 2nd Sess., 1977.

See esp. 93-110.

208. U.S. Congress. Senate. Judiciary Committee. Trotskyite Terrorist International, Hearings before the Sub-committee on Internal Security, July 24, 1975. 94th Cong., 1st Sess., 1976.

209. U.S. Congress. Senate. Judiciary Committee. The Terrorist and His Victim, Hearings July 21, 1977. 95th Cong., 1st Sess., 1977.

210. U.S. Congress. Senate. Judiciary Committee.
     Panama Canal and the Problem of Security.
     Committee Print, 94th Cong., 42nd Sess.,
     October 1976.

211. U.S. Congress. Senate. Judiciary Committee.
     Implementing International Conventions
     Against Terrorism, Senate Report 94-1273,
     September 26, 1976. 94th Cong., 2nd
     Sess., 1976.

212. U.S. Congress. Senate. Judiciary Committee.
     Threats to the Peaceful Observance of the
     Bicentennial, Hearings, June 18, 1976.
     94th Cong., 2nd Sess., 1976.

213. U.S. Congress. Senate. Judiciary Committee.
     Terroristic Activity: Interlock Between
     Communism and Terrorism, Part 9, Hearings
     Before the Sub-committee on Internal Se-
     curity, March 7, 1976. 94th Cong., 2nd
     Sess., 1976.

     Includes testimony by a former terrorist,
     data on the Weather Underground, Black Libera-
     tion Army, SLA, New World Liberation Front, and
     the FALN. List of terrorist activities from
     1965-1970 is appended.

214. U.S. Congress. Senate. Judiciary Committee.
     Puerto Rican Workers Organization. Commit-
     tee Print, March 1976. 94th Cong., 2nd
     Sess., 1976.

215. U.S. Congress. Senate. Judiciary Committee.
     Terroristic Activity: Terrorist Bombings
     and Law Enforcement Intelligence, Part 7,
     Hearings Before the Sub-committee on Inter-
     nal Security, October 23, 1975. 94th Cong.,
     1st Sess., 1975.

216. U.S. Congress. Senate. Judiciary Committee.
     Terroristic Activity, Part 4, International
     Terrorism, Hearings Before the Sub-commit-
     tee on Internal Security. 94th Cong., 1st
     Sess., May 14, 1975.

     Contains congressional research paper, "In-
     ternational Terrorism" by Vita Bite.

47

217. U.S. Congress. Senate. Judiciary Committee.
Terrorist Activity, Part 3, Hearings Before
the Sub-committee on Internal Security.
93rd Cong., 2nd Sess., July 5, 1974.

218. U.S. Congress. Senate. Judiciary Committee.
Terroristic Activity, Part 1, Hearings Before the Sub-committee on Internal Security. 93rd Cong., 2nd Sess., September 23,
1974.

219. U.S. Department of Justice. Terrorism--Its
Tactics and Techniques--An FBI Special
Study. Washington, D.C.: Government
Printing Office, January 12, 1973.

220. U.S. Department of Justice, Law Enforcement As-
sistance Administration. Disorders and
Terrorism: Report of the Task Force on
Disorders and Terrorism. Washington, D.C.:
Government Printing Office, 1976.

   While mainly intended for the law enforcement community, this bulky report (661 pp.)
deserves wider attention. Subjects include
terrorism in general, specific constabulary,
executive, and judicial concerns, nuclear
terror, and terrorism in its particular regional manifestations (viz. Germany, Argentina,
and Canada). Individual entries are provided
in this work for several of the contributions,
see A41 and H60. It is indexed. Special features: extensive bibliography and chronology.

221. U.S. Department of State. "Chronology of Attacks Upon Non-official American Citizens,
1971-1975." Washington D.C.: January 20,
1976.

222. U.S. Department of State. "Chronology of Sig-
nificant Terrorist Incidents Involving U.S.
Diplomatic Official Personnel, 1963-1975."
Washington, D.C.: January 20, 1976.

223. U.S. Department of State. Background Documen-
tation Relating to the Assassinations of
Ambassador Cleo A. Noel, Jr. and George
Curtis Moore. Washington: idem, 1973.

224. U.S. Department of State. State Department
Conference on Terrorism. U.S. Department
of State External Research Study,
XR/RNAS-21, December 29, 1972.

   Summary of the findings of a conference.

225. VanDelen, Hendrik. "Terror as a Political
     Weapon." Military Police Law Enforcement
     Journal, 2 (Spring 1975): 21-26.

226. Vance, Cyrus R. "Terrorism: Scope of the
     Threat and Needs for Effective Legislation."
     Department of State Bulletin, March 1978,
     53-55.

     The Secretary of State's statement before
     the Senate Committee on Governmental Affairs,
     January 23, 1978.

227. Walzer, Michael. Just and Unjust Wars: A
     Moral Argument with Historical Illustra-
     tions. New York: Basic Books, 1977.

     See esp. 197-206, wherein Walzer argues
     that the rather precise "political code" which
     demarcated protected persons from acceptable
     victims has seen a significant deterioration
     in the manifestations of contemporary terror-
     ism.

228. Walzer, Michael; Bell, J. Bowyer; and Morris,
     Roger. "Terrorism: A Debate." New Re-
     public, December 27, 1975, 12-15.

229. Waterman, D.A., and Jenkins, Brian M. Heuris-
     tic Modeling Using-Role-Based Computer
     Systems. Santa Monica, Calif.: Rand Cor-
     poration, 1977.

     Report of efforts to analyze international
     terrorist activities through a computer-based
     program.

230. Watson, Francis M. Political Terrorism: The
     Threat and the Response. Washington:
     Robert B. Luce Co., Inc., 1976.

     A popular treatment for the unsophistica-
     ted reader. An Appendix (24 pp.) listing sig-
     nificant incidents of terrorism, and 97 organi-
     zations that practice terrorism is too incom-
     plete to be of much value to the specialist.

231. Wilkinson, Paul. Terrorism and the Liberal
     State. New York: John Wiley & Sons, 1977.

A work which borders on the elegant, particularly with Wilkinson's treatment of the foundations of the liberal state. Wilkinson attempts to balance the obligations of the state to the individual, with the doctrines of government, law and authority. Although he is identified with the "law and order" school of thought, Wilkinson concedes that those who are denied the rights of citizenship cannot be morally bound to obey the dictum of the state. Although marred by a few errors, in particular with regard to the Middle East, this work stands far above the typical work in the field.

232. _____. Political Terrorism. New York: John Wiley & Sons, 1974.

An exceptional general treatment of political terrorism. Wilkinson has provided an historically informed work, which combines a competent treatment of the 19th century origins modern terrorism with a discussion of its contemporary manifestations. Wilkinson's succinct analysis of terrorism is complemented with some masterful syntheses of the more important works in the field (and adjacent fields of study). Wilkinson proffers an "elementary typology of political terrorism" which distinguishes between revolutionary, sub-revolutionary and repressive variants; however, he fails to provide a discernible basis for identifying revolutionary vis-a-vis sub-revolutionary terrorism, but this is only a minor demerit in an otherwise useful and informative book. A relatively extensive (157 entries) bibliography is provided.

233. _____. "Three Questions on Terrorism." Government and Opposition, 8 (Summer 1973): 290-312.

234. Winegarten, Renee. "Literary Terrorism." Commentary, March 1974, 58-65.

235. Wolf, John B. "Terrorist Manipulation of the Democratic Process." Police Journal (England), 48 (April-June 1975): 102-112.

(unseen)

236. _____. "Organization and Management Prac-
     tices of Urban Terrorist Groups." _Terror-
     ism_ (1978): 169-186.

     A discussion of the cellular organizational
framework utilized by terrorists. Unusually
well-informed.

237. _____. "Urban Terrorist Operations." _Po-
     lice Journal_ (England), 49 (October-Decem-
     ber 1976): 277-284.

     Wolf cites the Tupamaros as an example of
successful urban terrorists.

238. _____. "Analytical Framework for the Study
     and Control of Agitational Terrorism."
     Police Journal (England), 49 (July-Septem-
     ber 1976): 165-171.

     (unseen)

239. Zinam, Oleg. "Terrorism and Violence in the
     Light of a Theory of Discontent and Frus-
     tration." In Entry A117, 240-265.

Dalen, Hendrik van. "Terrorism and Human Na-
    ture." Military Police Law Enforcement
    Journal, Summer 1979, 9-14.

Kupperman, Robert H., and Trent, Darrell M.
    Terrorism: Threat, Reality, Response.
    Stanford, CA: Hoover Institution Press,
    Stanford University, 1979.

This book contains about 180 pages of original material with eight selected readings.
Kupperman and Trent treat the possibility of
"nationally disruptive terrorism", as well as
the appropriate government response to such
acts. Walter Laqueur has contributed a ten
page preface to the book, and a twelve page
bibliography is included. Kupperman is the
Chief Scientist for the Arms Control and Disarmament Agency.

Royal United Services Institute (RUSI) for De-
    fense Studies. Ten Years of Terrorism:
    Collected Views. New York: Crane, Russak,
    & Co., Inc., 1979.

Despite some sloppy editing, this book has
managed to emerge as a notably lucid discussion
of terrorism. The book is the result of a lec-
ture series conducted throughout 1977 at the
RUSI. While the contributions tend to address
British concerns, there remains much of interest
to the non-British reader. As might be expected, Northern Ireland is the major focus of Ten
Years of Terrorism; however, the reader will
also find that the space devoted to the media
and terrorism is particularly revealing, both
in the nature of the Northern Ireland problem,
and in the pathology of terrorism in general.
Contributors include: Martin Bell, Max Beloff,
Lord Caradon, Richard Clutterbuck, and Sir
Richard Thompson.

Simp, Howard R. "Terror." U.S. Naval Insti-
    tute Proceedings, 96 (1970): 64-69.

Section B
Related Works

1. Arendt, Hannah. On Revolution. New York: Viking, 1965.

2. Camus, Albert. The Rebel: An Essay on Man in Revolt. Translated by Anthony Bower, with a Foreward by Herbert Read. New York: Vintage Books, 1956.

3. Chakhotin, S. The Rape of the Masses. New York: Haskell, 1971.

4. Chappell, Duncan, and Monahan, John, eds. Violence and Criminal Justice. Lexington, Mass.: Lexington Books, D.C. Heath, 1975.

5. Cohen, A.S. Theories of Revolution: An Introduction. New York: A Halstead Press Book, John Wiley and Sons, 1975.

6. Cross, James E. Conflict in the Shadows. New York: Doubleday, 1963.

7. Curtis, Lynn A. Violence, Race and Culture. Lexington, Mass.: Lexington Books, 1975.

8. Dadrian, V. "Factors of Anger and Aggression in Genocide." Journal of Human Relations, 19 (1971): 394-417.

9. Dahlgren, Harold E. Profile of Violence: An Analytical Model. Washington, D.C.: Central Intelligence Agency (PR 76 10025), June 1976.

10. Dasgupta, S. "Violence: Development and Tensions." International Journal of Group

Tensions, 1 (1971): 114-129.

11. Davies, James C. "Toward a Theory of Revolu-
    tion." American Sociological Review, 27
    (1962): 5-14.

12. Davies, James C., ed. When Men Revolt and Why.
    New York: Free Press, 1971.

13. Dionisopoulog, P. Allen. Rebellion, Racism,
    and Representation. DeKalb: Northern
    Illinois Univ. Press, 1970.

14. Dollard, John. Frustration and Aggression.
    New Haven: Yale Univ. Press, 1969.

15. Downton, James V. Rebel Leadership: Committ-
    ment and Charisma in the Revolutionary
    Process. New York: Free Press, 1973.

16. Eckstein, Harry, ed. Internal War. New York:
    Free Press, 1964.

17. Ellis, Albert, and Gullo, John. Murder and
    Assassination. New York: Stuart Lyle,
    1971.

18. Feierabend, I.K.; Feirabend, R.L.; and Nesvold,
    B. "Comparative Study of Revolution and
    Violence." Comparative Politics, 5 (April
    1973): 393-424.

19. Feierabend, I.K.; Feierabend, R.L.; and Gurr,
    T.R., eds. Anger, Violence and Politics:
    Theories and Research. Englewood Cliffs:
    Prentice Hall, 1972.

20. Firestone, Joseph M. "Continuities in the
    Theory of Violence." Journal of Conflict
    Resolution, 18 (1974): 117-133.

21. Friedrich, C.J. "Opposition and Government By
    Violence." Government and Opposition, 7
    (1972): 3-19.

22. Fromm, Erich. The Anatomy of Human Destruc-
    tiveness. New York: Rinehart & Winston,
    1973.

23. Greene, Thomas H. Comparative Revolutionary
    Movements. Englewood Cliffs, NJ: Prentice

Hall, 1974.

24. Gurr, Ted Robert. Why Men Rebel. Princeton, NJ: Princeton University Press, 1970.

25. Hachey, Thomas, ed. Voices of Revolution: Rebels and Rhetoric. Dryden Press, 1973.

26. Hacker, Andrew. "Dostoevsky's Disciples: Man and Sheep in Political Theory." Journal of Politics, 18 (1955): 590-613.

27. Hagopian, M.N. Phenomenon of Revolution. New York: Dodd, Mead and Company, 1975.

28. Hibbs, D.A., Jr. Mass Political Violence: A Cross: National Causal Analysis. New York: John Wiley and Sons, 1973.

29. Hobsbawn, E.J. Revolutionaries: Contemporary Essays. New York: Pantheon, 1973.

30. Huntington, Samuel. "Civil Violence and the Process of Development." Adelphi Papers, No. 83. London: International Institute for Strategic Studies, 1971.

31. Johnson, Chalmers. Revolutionary Change. Boston: Little, Brown and Company, 1966.

32. _____. Autopsy on People's War. Berkeley: University of California Press, 1973.

33. Kelman, Herbert C. "Violence Without Moral Restraint: Reflections on the Dehumanization of Victims and Victimizers." Journal of Social Issues, 29 (1973): 25-61.

34. Laqueur, Walter. Guerrilla: A Historical and Political Study. Boston: Little, Brown, 1976.

35. Larson, Otto, ed. Violence and the Mass Media. New York: Harper and Row, 1968.

36. Lasky, Melvin J. Utopia and Revolution: On the Origins of a Metaphor, or Some Illustrations of the Problem of Political Temperament and Intellectual Climate and How Ideas, Ideals, and Ideologies Have Been Historically Related. Chicago: University

Press, 1976.

37. Lasswell, Harold A., and Lerner, Daniel, eds. World Revolutionary Elites: Studies in Coercive Ideological Movements. Cambridge, Mass.: Massachusetts Institute of Technology Press, 1965.

38. Leiden, Carl., and Schmitt, Karl M., eds. The Politics of Violence. Englewood Cliffs, NJ: Prentice Hall, 1968.

39. Leites, Nathan, and Wolf, Charles, Jr. Rebellion and Authority: An Analytic Essay on Insurgent Conflicts. Chicago: Markham, Lieuwen, Edwin, 1970.

40. Liebert, Robert. Radical and Militant Youth: A Psychoanalytic Inquiry. New York: Praeger Publishers, 1971.

41. Lorenz, Konrad. On Aggression. Trans. by Marjorie Kerr Wilson. New York: Bantam Books, 1966.

42. Lowi, Theodore J. Politics of Disorder. New York: W.W. Norton, 1971.

43. Lupsha, Peter. "Explanation of Political Violence: Some Psychological Theories." Politics and Society, 2 (1971): 88-104.

44. Mars, P. "Nature of Political Violence." Social and Economic Studies (Kingston, Jamaica) 24 (June 1975): 221-238.

45. May, Rollo. Power and Innocence: A Search for the Sources of Violence. New York: Norton, 1972.

46. Mazlish, Bruce. The Revolutionary Ascetic: Evolution of a Political Type. New York: Basic Books, Inc., 1976.

    See esp. Part One, "Theory and Practice", 3-43.

47. Nieburg, M.L. Political Violence: The Behavioral Process. New York: St. Martin's Press, 1969.

48. Osanka, Franklin M. Modern Guerrilla Warfare:
    Fighting Communist Guerrilla Movements,
    1941-1961. New York: Free Press, 1962.

49. Parker, Guy J. Sources of Instability in Dev-
    eloping Countries. Santa Monica, Califor-
    nia: The Rand Corporation, publication
    P-5029, 1973.

50. Pepitone, Albert. "The Social Psychology of
    Violence." International Journal of Group
    Tensions, 2 (1972): 19-32.

51. Priestland, G. Future of Violence. London:
    Hamish Hamilton, Ltd., 1974.

52. Roucek, J.S. "Sociological Elements of a
    Theory of Terror and Violence." American
    Journal of Economics and Sociology, 21
    (April 1962): 165-172.

53. Sarkesian, Sam C., ed. Revolutionary Guerrilla
    Warfare. Chicago: Precedent, 1975.

54. Schelling, Thomas. The Strategy of Conflict.
    New York: Oxford University Press, 1963.

55. Short, J.F., and Wolfgang, M.E. Collective
    Violence. Chicago: Aldine, 1972.

56. Shulman, Alix K. Red Emma Speaks. New York:
    Random House, 1972.

57. Singh, Baljit: "Theory and Practice of Modern
    Guerrilla Warfare." New York: Asia
    Publishing House, 1971.

58. Skobnick, Jerome, ed. The Politics of Protest.
    New York: Ballantine, 1964.

59. Stolz, Matthew F., ed. Politics on the New
    Left. Beverly Hills: Glencoe Press, 1971.

60. Suchlicki, Jaime. University Students and Re-
    volution in Cuba, 1920-1968. Coral Gables,
    FL: University of Miami Press, 1969.

61. Taber, Robert. The War of the Flea: A Study of
    Guerrilla Warfare Theory and Practice. NY:
    Lyle Stuart, 1965.

62. Talmon, J.L. "The Legacy of Georges Sorel:
    Marxism, Violence, Fascism." Encounter,
    34 (February 1970): 47-60.

63. Tanter, Raymond, and Midlarsky, Manus. "A
    Theory of Revolution." Journal of Conflict
    Resolution, 9 (1967): 264ff.

64. Taylor, Charles L., and Hudson, Michael C.
    World Handbook of Political and Social In-
    dicators, 2nd ed. New Haven: Yale Uni-
    versity Press, 1972.

65. Thompson, Sir Robert. Defeating Communist In-
    surgency. London: Chatto and Windus,
    1966.

66. Venturi, Franco. Roots of Revolution. New
    York: Grosset & Dunlap, 1966.

67. Vox der Mekden, Fred R. Comparative Political
    Violence. Englewood Cliffs, NJ: Prentice
    Hall, 1973.

68. Waddis, Jack. New Theories of Revolution.
    New York: International Publishers, 1972.

69. Walzer, Michael. The Revolution of the Saints:
    A Study in the Origins of Radical Politics.
    Cambridge, Mass.: Harvard University Press,
    1965.

70. Wilber, Charles G., ed. Contemporary Violence:
    A Multi-disciplinary Examination. Spring-
    field, IL: Charles C. Thomas, 1975.

71. Wolfgang, Marvin E. and Ferranti, Franco. The
    Subculture of Violence: Toward an Inte-
    grated Theory in Criminology. London:
    Tavistock, 1967.

72. Woods, J. New Theories of Revolution: A Com-
    mentary on the Views of Frantz Fanon,
    Regis Debray, and Herbert Marcuse. New
    York: International Publishers, 1972.

73. Zwiebach, Burton. Civility and Disobedience.
    London: Cambridge University Press, 1975.

Section C
Philosophic, Ideologic, and Moral Foundations of Terrorism

1. Abdul, Haris Nasution. Fundamentals of Guerrilla Warfare. New York: Praeger, 1965.

2. Ali, Tariq, ed. The New Revolutionaries: A Handbook of the International Radical Left. New York: William Morrow and Company, 1969.

   Collection of materials by prominent student anarchists and leftists.

3. Arendt, Hannah. On Violence. New York: Harcourt, Brace & World, Inc., 1969, 1970.

   An important essay notable on a number of counts including Arendt's distinction between terror and violence: "Terror is not the same as violence; it is rather, the form of government that comes into being when violence having destroyed all power, does not abdicate but, on the contrary, remains in full control."

4. Bayo Giroud, Alberto. 150 Questions to a Guerrilla. Boulder, Colorado: Panther, 1963.

5. Bern, H.Von Dach. Total Resistance. Boulder, Colorado: Panther Publications, 1965.

6. Camus, Albert. Neither Victims Nor Executioners. Chicago: World Without War, 1968.

   (unseen)

7. Cranston, Maurice W. The New Left: Six Critical Essays on Che Guevara, Jean-Paul

Sartre, Herbert Marcuse, Frantz Fanon, Black Power, R. D. Laing. New York: The Library Press, 1971.

8. Daniel, James, ed. The Complete Bolivian Diaries of Che Guevara and Other Captured Documents. New York: Stein and Day, 1968.

9. Deakin, Thomas J. "The Legacy of Carlos Marighella." FBI Law Enforcement Bulletin, October 1974, 1-7.

10. Debray, Regis. Revolution in the Revolution. New York: Grove Press, 1967.

Reprint of the original essay published in the Monthly Review, 3 (July-August 1967).

11. _____. Che's Guerrilla War. London: Penquin Books, 1969.

An admirer's account.

12. Ellul, Jacques. Violence: Reflections From a Christian Perspective, trans. by Cecilia Gaul. New York: Seabury, 1969.

13. Fanon, Frantz. The Wretched of the Earth. New York: Grove Press, 1967.

Fanon's influential book is especially notable for his identification of violence as a "cleansing force," as a means of freeing the oppressed from their complexes, their dispair and their inaction. Sartre's espousal of the liberating role of violence may be found in the extended preface.

14. Gendzier, Irene L. Franz Fanon: A Critical Study. New York: Pantheon Books, 1973.

15. Gerassi, John, ed. Venceramos: The Speeches and Writing of Che Guevara. London: Panther, 1968.

16. Guevara, Ernesto Che. Episodes of the Revolutionary War. New York: International Publishers, 1968.

17. _____. Reminiscences of the Cuban Revolutionary War, trans. by V. Ortiz. New York:

Monthly Review Press, 1968.

18. _____. Guerrilla Warfare. New York: Random House, 1965.

19. Hansen, Emmanuel. Frantz Fanon: Social and Political Thought. Columbus, Ohio: Ohio State University Press, 1976.

20. Ho Chi Minh. On Revolution. New York: Praeger, 1967.

21. Hodges, Donald C., ed. Philosophy of the Urban Guerrilla: The Revolutionary Writings of Abraham Guillen. New York: Morrow, 1973.

    Includes translations of "the Strategy of Urban Warfare," "the Theory of Violence," and "the Rebellion of the Third World." This important volume is useful for gaining an appreciation of the urban as opposed to the rural forces.

22. Hoffer, Eric. The True Believer: Thoughts on the Nature of Mass Movements. New York: Harper and Row, Publishers, 1951.

    The True Believer is an insightful, often brilliant essay examining the mass movement phenomenon. Many of Hoffer's observations are equally applicable to terrorists and non-terrorist organizations. He finds the membership of such groups is likely to be drawn from the ranks of the frustrated (including the poor, the misfits, the bored and the selfish), who when combined with the proper conditions, and the indispensible outstanding leader, coagulate into the mass movement. Hoffer's treatment has survived nearly 30 years in the intellectual marketplace almost intact; clear evidence of the value of this little book.

23. Honerich, Ted. Political Violence. Ithaca, NY: Cornell University Press, 1977.

    A philosophic disquisition.

24. Hook, Sidney. "The Ideology of Violence." Encounter, April 1970, 26-38.

The resort to violence in a democratic society is seen as an affront to democracy, an
attempt to subvert majority rule, by minority
tyranny. Hook develops the distinction between legitimate force and illegitimate violence; he decries the growing acceptance of
violence. He concludes that the fear of violence may affect change, but he finds that the
exercise of violence may have the opposite effect. Hook herein reprints "In Defense of
Terrorism" by R.E. Hyland. The Harvard Crim-
son, October 22, 1969.

25. Huberman, Leo, and Sweezy, Paul M., eds. Regis
     Debray and the Latin American Revolution.
     New York: Monthly Review Press, 1968.

26. Kutner, Luis. "A Philosophical Perspective on
     Rebellion." In Entry A12, 51-64.

27. Levy, Bernard-Henri. "The War Against All."
     The New Republic, February 11, 1978, 14-18.

     Neo-Marxist critique of terrorism. Depict-
ing terrorism as the dialectic between the
state terrorist and the individual terrorist.
The individual terrorist seeking to dominate
the state and taking the masses as his victim.
Levy is one of the Nouveaux philosophes.

28. Mallin, Jay, ed. Strategy for Conquest: Com-
     munist Documents on Guerrilla Warfare.
     Coral Gables, FL: University of Miami
     Press, 1970.

     Includes material by prominent guerrilla
strategists, some of which appear here for the
first time in English. Selections by Mao,
Giap, Guevara, Lin Piao, Raul Castro, et. al.

29. _____. Terror and Urban Guerrillas: A
     Study of Tactics and Documents. Coral
     Gables, FL: University of Miami Press,
     1971.

     Includes a number of important sources, in
particular Marighella's Minimanual and Bayo
Giroud's 150 Questions, as well as selections
by Lenin, Prosser, Arafat, and the Viet Cong.

30. Mao Tse-Tung. Basic Tactics. New York: Prae-
    ger, 1966.

31. _____ . On Guerrilla Warfare. New York:
    Praeger, 1961.

32. _____ . Selected Military Writing. Peking:
    1963.

33. Marcuse, Herbert. Eros and Civilization. Bos-
    ton: Beacon Press, 1955.

34. _____ . One Dimensional Man: Studies in the
    Ideology of Advanced Industrial Society.
    (Boston: Beacon Press, 1964).

35. _____ . An Essay on Liberation. Boston:
    Beacon Press, 1969.

    Marcuse calls for rebellion against "estab-
    lished legality: An opposition which is direc-
    ted, not against a particular form of govern-
    ment or against particular conditions within a
    society, but against a given society as a whole,
    cannot remain legal and lawful because it is
    the established legality and the established
    law that it opposes."

36. _____ . Five Lectures, trans. by Jeremy J.
    Shapiro and Shierry Weber. Boston: Bea-
    con Press, 1970.

    A series of lectures presented in Berlin.
    See especially: "The Problem of Violence and
    the Radical Opposition," 83-108.

37. _____ . Counter-revolution and Revolt. Bos-
    ton: Beacon Press, 1972.

38. Marighella, Carlos. For the Liberation of
    Brazil. Harmondsworth: Penquin, 1972.

39. _____ . "Minimanual of the Urban Guerrilla."
    Tricontinental (Havana), 16 (January-Feb-
    ruary 1970): 15-56.

    Reprinted in Entry A139.

40. Nkrumah, Kwave. Handbook of Revolutionary
    Warfare. New York: International Pub-

lishers, 1972.

41. Sanford, R. Nevitt and Comstock, Craig, eds.
    Sanctions for Evil (San Francisco: Jos-
    sey-Bass, 1971).

    (unseen)

42. Sorel, Georges. Reflections on Violence.
    Trans. by T. E. Hulme and J. Roth. Intro-
    duction by Edward A. Shils. New York:
    Collier Books, 1950.

43. Strickler, Nina. "Anti-History and Terrorism:
    A Philosophical Dimension." In Bassiouni,
    ed., 47-50.

44. Trotsky, Leon. The Defense of Terrorism.
    London: George Allen and Unwin, 1921.

45. _____. The Defense of Terrorism--Terrorism
    and Communism: A Reply to Karl Kautsky.
    London: George Allen and Unwin, 1935.

46. _____. Terrorism and Communism. Ann
    Arbor: University of Michigan Press, 1961.

47. _____. Against Individual Terrorism. New
    York: Pathfinder Press, April, 1974.

    Excerpts and reprints of Trotsky's writings
    on the subject of terrorism. Including: "On
    Terrorism" (1911), "The Collapse of Terror and
    its Party" (1909), Trotsky's replies to Stal-
    in's accusations (1937), and a 1939 discussion
    of the futility of assassination.

48. Troung Chinh. Primer for Revolt. New York:
    Praeger, 1963.

49. Vo Nguyen Giap. Big Victory, Great Task. New
    York: Praeger, 1968.

50. _____. People's War, People's Army. New
    York: Praeger, 1967.

Section D
Anarchy and Nihilism: Key Works

Note to the reader: There is a veritable plethora of works on anarchism and nihilism. Rather
than move too far beyond the central subject of the
bibliography, the editors determined that the best
approach would be to provide the citations for the
central works on anarchism and nihilism. The inter-
ested user will find these works a good beginning,
and the annotations indicate those books which contain noteworthy bibliographies as a tool for further
research.

See also: "Biography," Section E.

1. Avrich, Paul. The Russian Anarchists. New
   York: W. W. Norton & Co., 1978.

   The text of the 1967 edition (Princeton) with
   minor revisions and an updated (32 pp.) bibliography. Clearly the best work on the subject
   currently available.

2. Bakunin, Michael. God and the State. New York:
   Dover Publications, Inc., 1970. Original
   publication 1916.

   Paul Avrich, the noted authority on anarchism, has provided a brief (9 pp.) introduction
   to this classic work on anarchism. A new index
   has been added by the publisher.

3. Bakunin, Michael and Nachayev, Sergei. The
   Revolutionary Catechism.

   (unseen)

   Reprinted in: Michael Confino, ed. Daughter

of a Revolutionary. London: Alcove Press,
1974.

4. Baldwin, Roger N., ed. Kropotkins Revolutionary
    Pamphlets: A Collection of Writings by Peter
    Kropotkin. New York: Dover Publications,
    1970.

    A republication of the original 1927 Vanguard
    edition. Includes some 37 pages of introductory
    and biographical materials on Kropotkin. In-
    cludes the following works: "The Spirit of
    Revolt," "Anarchist Communism," "Anarchist Mor-
    ality," "Revolutionary Government," "Anarchism"
    (the article prepared by Kropotkin for the 1905
    edition of The Encyclopedia Britannica), et. al.

5. Berkman, Alexander. Now and After: The A.B.C.
    of Communist Anarchism. New York: Vanguard,
    1929.

6. Goldman, Emma. Anarchism and Other Essays. New
    York: Dover Publications, Inc. 1969.

    A republication of the original 1917 edition.
    A brief, nine-page introduction by Richard Drin-
    non has been added. Of particular note to the
    student of terrorism are Goldman's essays on the
    meaning of anarchism and the "psychology of po-
    litical violence."

7. Government and Opposition: A Journal of Compar-
    ative Politics (London), Autumn, 1970.

    (unseen)

    Theme issue devoted to contemporary anar-
    chism.

8. Harbold, William H. Review of several works by
    Bakunin, Goldman and Kropotkin. American
    Political Science Review 72 (June 1978):
    646-649.

    An excellent and succinct review article.

9. Hoffman, Robert, ed. Anarchism. New York:
    Atherton Press, 1970.

    An introductory reader with selections by
    Proudhon, Goldman, Berkman, Joll, Bertrand

Russell, et. al. The selections are carefully chosen to minimize obtuseness and complexity.

10. Horowitz, Irving L., ed. The Anarchists. New York: Dell Publishing, 1964.

11. Horowitz, Irving L. Foundations of Political Sociology. New York: Harper & Row, Publishers, 1972.

    See esp. chap. 8, "Anarchism: From Natural Man to Political Man," pp. 148-186. Includes selected bibliography.

12. Joll, James. The Anarchists. Boston: Little, Brown and Company, 1964.

    Rivals Woodcock's Anarchism as the best work on the subject.

13. Lum, Dyer D. A Concise History of the Great Trial of the Chicago Anarchists. Chicago: Socialistic Publishing Co., 1886.

    (unseen)

14. Most, Johann. The Beast of Property. New Haven: International Workingman's Association Group, 1883.

15. _____. Science of Revolutionary War: Manual for Instructions in the Use and Preparation of Nitro-Glycerine, Dynamite, Gun-Cotton, Fulminating Mercury, Bombs, Fuses, and Poisons, etc. New York: International Zeitung Verein, 1884.

16. Proudhon, Pierre J. What is Property?: An Enquiry Into the Principle and Right of Government. New York: Dover Publications, ca. 1970.

    Republication of the 1876 edition.

17. Shatz, Marshall S., ed. The Essential Works of Anarchism. New York: Quadrangle Books, 1972.

    A very exceptional reader including key sources by Godwin, Stirner, Proudhon, Bakunin, Kropotkin, Tolstoy, Goldman, Berkman,

Rocker, et. al.

18. Stirner, Max (Johann Caspar Schmidt). The Ego
    and its Own. Trans. by S. T. Byington.
    London: Fifield, 1907.

19. Woodcock, George. Anarchism: A History of
    Libertarian Ideas and Movements. Cleveland:
    Meridian Books, The World Publishing Company,
    1962.

    The essential source on the subject. In-
    cludes a selected bibliography.

20. _____. "Anarchism Revisited." Commentary
    August 1968, pp. 54-60.

    The revival of anarchism in the 1960's.

Section E
Biography

(Note, biographic materials are also contained in
appropriate topical sections.)

1. Berkman, Alexander. Prison Memoirs of an Anar-
    chist. Pittsburgh, 1970; New York:
    Schocken, 1970.

    Republication of the 1926 edition.

2. Carr, Edward M. Michael Bakunin. New York:
    Vintage, 1961.

    The standard work on Bakunin.

3. Davis, Angela. An Autobiography. New York:
    Random House, 1974.

4. Goldman, Emma. Living My Life. New York:
    New American Library, 1977.

    Originally published in 1931, this is the
    autobiography of the famous anarchist. She
    treats political violence episodically. This
    edition includes a brief bibliographic essay,
    and a new considerably improved index. An
    unabridged republication is also available,
    in two volumes, from Dover Publications of
    New York.

5. Khaled, Leila. My People Shall Live: the
    Autobiography of a Revolutionary. London:
    Hodder and Stoughton, 1973.

6. Kropotkin, Peter. Memoirs of a Revolutionist.
    New York: Houghton Mifflin, 1899.

    Republished by Dover Publications of New
    York, (1971) with a 17 page introduction by
    Nicolar Walter, who has also provided nearly

40 pages of very useful notes to the text. A very readable political memoir.

7. Miller, Martin A. _Kropotkin_. Chicago: University of Chicago Press, 1976.

8. Powers, Thomas. _Diana: The Makings of a Terrorist_. New York: 1971.

9. Savinkov, B.V. _Memoirs of a Terrorist_. New York: Kraus Reprint, 1970.

10. Sinclair, Andrew. _Guevera_. London: Fontana/ Collins, 1970.

11. Stern, Susan. _With the Weathermen_. Garden City, NY: Doubleday & Co., 1975.

   An insider's account by a minor leader. The especially illuminating aspect of Ms. Stern's book is that she never tells the reader why she joined the Weathermen, and one suspects there is not a very profound explanation or motive. More than anything else her involvement with violent left seems to have been a trip, and indeed she states (p.3): "It was rare that I wasn't stoned. . ."

12. Vallieres, Pierre. _White Niggers of America: the Precocious Autobiography of a Quebec Terrorist_. New York: Monthly Review Press, 1971.

Section F
Legal Perspectives

Note: additional materials are also contained
       in appropriate topical sections in section
       G (Tactics).

1. Abu-Lughad, Ibrahim. "Unconventional Violence
    and International Law." American Journal
    of International Law, 67 (November 1973):
    100-104.

2. Bailey, Sydney D. Prohibitions and Restraints
    in War. London: Oxford University Press,
    1972.

3. Bassiouni, M. Cherif. "The Political Offense
    Exception in Extradition Law and Practice."
    In Entry A12, 398-447.

4. _____. "Methodological Options for Inter-
    national Legal Control of Terrorism."
    In Entry A12, 485-492.

5. Baxter, R. R. "Skeptical Look at the Concept
    of Terrorism." Akron Law Review, 7
    (Spring 1974): 380-87.

6. Blishchenko, I.P. "International Violence as
    a Special Problem of the Fight Against
    Crime." International Review of Criminal
    Policy, 32 (1976): 8-13.

7. Bond, James E. The Rules of Riot: Internal
    Conflict and the Law of War. Princeton,
    NJ: Princeton University Press, 1974.

8. Cantrell, C.L. "Political Offense Exemption
    in International Extradition: A Comparison
    of the United States, Great Britain and the
    Republic of Ireland." Marquette Law
    Review, 60 (1977): 777-824.

9. De Schutter, Bart. "Problems of Jurisdiction in the International Control and Repression of Terrorism." In Entry A12, 377-390.

10. Dugard, John. "International Terrorism: Problems of Definition." International Affairs, 50 (January 1974): 67-81.

11. Evans, Alona E. "The Realities of Extradition and Prosecution." A paper presented to the Conference on International Terrorism, Ralph Bunche Institute, Graduate School and University Center of CUNY, and the State University College at Oneonta of SUNY, June 9-11, 1976. Also, pp. 128-138 Entry A4.

12. Evans, Alona E., and Murphy, John F. "Legal Aspects of International Terrorism: the Trees and the Forest." In An Act to Combat International Terrorism, 526-554.

13. Falk, Richard A. "The Beirut Raid and the International Law of Retaliation." American Journal of International Law, 63 (July 1969): 415-443.

14. _____. "Terror, Liberation Movements, and the Processes of Social Change." American Journal of International Law, 63 (1969): 423-427.

15. Franck, Thomas M. "International Legal Action Concerning Terrorism." Terrorism, I (1978): 187-197.

16. Franck, Thomas M., and Lockwood, Bert B ., Jr. "Preliminary Thoughts Toward an International Convention on Terrorism." The American Journal of International Law, 68 (January 1974): 69-90.

17. Friedlander, Robert A. "Terrorism and International Law: What is Being Done?" Rutgers Camden Law Journal, 8 (Spring 1977): 383-392.

18. Garcia-Mora, Manuel R. "The Present Status of Political Offenses in the Law of Extradition and Asylum." University of Pittsburgh Law Review, 14 (1953).

19. _____. "The Nature of Political Offenses: A Knotty Problem of Extradition Law." Virginia Law Review, 48 (1962).

20. _____. International Responsibility for Hostile Acts of Private Persons Against Foreign States. The Hague: Martinus Nijhoff, 1962.

21. _____. "Crimes Against Humanity and the Principle of Non-Extradition of Political Offenses." Michigan Law Review, 62 (1964)

22. Green, L.C. "International Law and the Suppression of Terrorism," edited by G.W. Bartholomew. Malaya Law Review Legal Essays, 1975.

23. Hannay, William A. "International Terrorism: the Need for a Fresh Perspective." International Lawyer, 8 (1974): 268-284.

24. Khan, Muhammed Zafrulla. "Asylum--Article 14 of the Universal Declaration." Journal of the International Commission of Jurists, 8 (1967).

25. Khan, Rahmatullah. "Guerrilla Warfare and International Law." International Studies (New Delhi), 9 (October 1967).

26. Kittrie, N.N. "New Look at Political Offenses and Terrorism." In Criminology in Perspective: Essays in Honor of Israel Drapkin edited by S.F. Landau. Lexington, MA: Heath Lexington Books, 1977.

27. Kuhn, Arthur K. "The Complaint of Yugoslavia Against Hungary with Reference to the Assassination of King Alexander." American Journal of International Law, 29 (1935): 87-92.

28. Kutner, Luis. "Constructive Notice: A Proposal to End International Terrorism." New York Law Forum, 19 (Fall 1973): 325-350.

29. Lador-Lederer, J.J. "A Legal Approach to International Terrorism." Israel Law Review, 9 (1974): 194-220.

30. Lauterpacht, Hans. "Revolutionary Activities by Persons Against Foreign States." _American Journal of International Law_, 22 (1928): 105-130.

31. "The Law of Limited International Conflict." (Georgetown University, Washington, D.C.: Institute of World Policy, April 1965).

32. Layey, Kathleen A., and Sang, Lewis M. "Control of Terrorism Through a Broader Interpretation of Article 3 of the Four Geneva Conventions of 1949." In Entry A12, 191-200.

33. Lillich, R.B., and Carbonneau, T.E. "Terrorism Amendment (1976) to the Foreign Assistance Act of 1961." _Journal of International Law and Economics_, 2 (1977): 223-236.

34. Lillich, R.B., and Paxman, J.M. "State Responsibility for Injuries Occasioned by Terrorist Activities." _American University Law Review_, 26 (Winter 1977): 217-313.

35. Lockwood, Bert. "The Utility of International Law in Dealing with International Terrorism." Paper presented to the International Studies Association Convention, Washington, D.C., February 20, 1975.

36. Mallison, W.T., Jr., and Mallison, S.N. "The Concept of Public Purpose Terror in International Law." _Howard Law Journal_, 18 (1973): 12-28. See also _Journal of Palestine Studies_, 4 (Winter 1975): 36-51.

37. Moore, J.W. "Terrorism and Political Crimes in International Law." _American Journal of International Law_, 67 (1973).

38. Moore, John Norton. "Towards Legal Restraints on International Terrorism." _Proceedings of the American Society of International Law_ (1973): 88-94.

39. Murphy, John F. "International Legal Controls of International Terrorism: Performance and Prospects." _Illinois Bar Journal_, 63 (April 1975): 444-452.

40. Palmer, Bruce. "Codification of Terrorism as an International Crime." In Entry A12, 507-518.

41. Paust, Jordan J. "Terrorism and the International Law of War." Military Law Review, 64 (Spring 1974): 1-36.

42. _____. "Terrorism and the International Law of War." Milwaukee Law Review, 64 (1974).

43. _____. "A Survey of Possible Legal Responses to International Terrorism: Prevention, Punishment and Cooperative Action." Georgia Journal of International and Comparative Law, 5 (1975).

44. _____. "Approach to Decision with Regard to Terrorism." Akron Law Review, 7 (Spring 1978): 397-403.

45. Radovanovic, Ljubomir. "The Problem of International Terrorism." Review of International Affairs, 23 (Belgrade), (October 1972): pp. 6-8, 5-20.

46. Rauch, Elmar. "The Compatibility of the Detention of Terrorists Order (Northern Ireland) with the European Convention for the Protection of Human Rights." New York University Journal of International Law and Politics, 6 (1973, Spring), 1-27.

47. Roux, J.A. "Le Projet de Convention Internationale pour la Repression des Crimes Presentant un Danger Public." Revue Internationale de Droit Penal, 12 (1935): 99-130.

48. Rovine, Arthur W. "The Contemporary International Legal Attack on Terrorism." Israel Journal on Human Rights, 3 (1973): 9-38.

49. Rubin, Alfred P. "International Terrorism and International Law." In Entry A4, 121-127.

50. Schwarzenberger, Georg. "Terrorists, Hijackers, Guerrilleros and Mercenaries." Current Legal Problems, 24 (1971): 257-282.

51. Shearer, I.A. Extradition in International Law
     (Dobbs Ferry: Oceana; Manchester: Manches-
     ter University Press, 1971).

52. Shepard, Ira M. "Air Piracy: The Role of the
     International Federation of Airline Pilots
     Associations." Cornell International Law
     Journal, 3 (1970): 79-91.

53. Sliwowski, George. "Legal Aspects of Terror-
     ism." In Entry A33.

54. Sundberg, M. Jacob. "Piracy: Sea and Air."
     International Law Association. Report of
     the Fifty-Fourth Conference (The Hague,
     August 23-29, 1970). London, 1971, 755-71.

55. Synge, T. M. "The Problem of Prisoners in
     Future Warfare." Royal United Service
     Institute, 77 (1932), 120-123.

56. Taulbee, J.L. "Retaliation and Irregular War-
     fare, in Contemporary International Law."
     International Lawyer (Chicago), 7 (January
     1973): 195-204.

57. "Terrorism and Political Crimes in Internation-
     al Law." (three papers, plus comments,
     discussion) American Journal of Interna-
     tional Law, 67 (November 1973): 87-111.

58. Tharp, Paul A., Jr. "The Laws of War as a
     Potential Legal Regime for the Control of
     Terrorist Activities." Journal of Inter-
     national Affairs, 32 (Spring/Summer 1978):
     91-100.

59. Toman, Jiri. "Terrorism and the Regulation of
     Armed Conflict." In Entry A12, 133-154.

60. United States. "Terrorism: the Proposed United
     States Draft Convention." Georgia Journal
     of International and Comparative Law, 3,
     no. 2 (1973): 430-447.

61. Vogler, Theo. "Perspectives on Extradition and
     Terrorism." In Entry A12, 391-397.

62. Wilson, Clifton E. Diplomatic Privileges and
     Immunities (Tucson, Arizona: University of
     Arizona Press, 1967): 51-62.

63. Woetzel, Robert K. "The Potential Role of an International Criminal Court." In <u>International Terrorism: Proceedings of an Intensive Panel at the 15th Annual Convention of the International Studies Association</u> (Institute of World Affairs, University of Wisconsin, Milwaukee, 1974): 73-84.

64. Zlataric, Bogdan. "History of International Terrorism and its Legal Control." In Entry A12, 474-484.

65. Zubkowski, L. Kos-Rabcewicz. "The Creation of an International Criminal Court." In Entry A12, 519-536.

Section G
Tactics

The reader is advised to consult both the
appropriate topical section (viz. Skyjacking) and
the appropriate regional section (viz. Middle East).

1. Powell, W. The Anarchist Cookbook. New York:
       Lyle Stuart, 1971.

       A how-to manual for the aspiring terrorist:
    From garrote to bomb.

1. ASSASSINATION

1. Abrahamson, David. The Murdering Mind. New
    York: Harper Colophon, 1973.

2. Barrett, R. T. "Political Assassination in
    Japan". Great Britain and the East, 50
    (March 10, 1938): 260.

    (unseen)

3. Bell, J. Bowyer. "Assassination in Interna-
    tional Politics: Lord Moyne, Count Berna-
    dotte and the Lehi." International Studies
    Quarterly, 16 (March 1972): 59-82.

4. Crotty, William J., ed. Assassinations and the
    Political Order. New York: Harper S. Row,
    1971.

5. Ellis, Albert, and Gullo, John. Murder and
    Assassination. New York: Lyle Stuart,
    1971.

6. Gribble, Leonard. Hands of Terror: Notable
    Assassinations of the 20th Century. Lon-
    don: Frederick Muller Ltd., 1960.

7. Gross, Feliks. "Political Assassination."
    In Entry A117, 307-315.

8. Hassel, Conrad V. "The Political Assassin."
    Journal of Police Science and Administra-
    tion, December 1974.

9. Havens, Murray C.; Leiden, Carl; Schmitt, Karl
    M. The Politics of Assassination. Engle-
    wood Cliffs, NJ: Prentice-Hall, 1970.

10. Havens, Murray C. "Assassination, Violence, and National Policy." A paper presented at the 1976 Conference of the Section on Military Studies of the International Studies Association.

Assassination (and other violence) as an instrument of national policy against other governments is examined, and Havens concludes that such tactics are rarely appropriate (if ever).

11. Hurwood, Bernhardt J. Society and the Assassin: A Background Book on Political Murder. New York: Parent's Magazine Press, 1970.

12. Hyams, Edward. Killing No Murder. New York: Panther, 1970. Original British edition published by Nelson in 1969.

13. Johnson, Francis. Famous Assassinations of History from Philip of Macedon, 336 B.C. to Alexander of Serbia, A.D. 1903. Chicago: A.C. McClurg and Co., 1903.

14. Kaplan, John. "The Assassins." Stanford Law Review, 5 (May 1967): 1110-1151.

15. Kelly, Joseph B. "Assassination in War Time." Military Law Review, 30 (October 1965): 101-111.

16. Kirkham, James F.; Levy, Sheldon G.; and Crotty, William J. Assassination and Political Violence: A Staff Report to the National Commission on the Causes and Prevention of Violence. New York: Bantam, 1970.

17. Leiden, Carl. "Assassination in the Middle East." Trans-Action, May 1969, 20-23.

18. Lerner, Max. "Assassination." Encyclopedia of the Social Sciences. New York: Mac Millan, 1930, 271-275.

19. Lewis, Bernard. The Assassins: A Radical Sect in Islem. New York: Basic Books, 1968.

20. Mac Donald, Arthur. "Assassins of Rulers."

Journal of the American Institute of Criminal Law and Criminology, 2 (November 1911): 505-520.

21. Marshall, John. "The 20th Century Vehme: Terror by Assassination." Blackwoods Magazine, June 1945, 421-425.

(unseen)

22. Mazrui, Ali A. "Thoughts on Assassination in Africa." Political Science Quarterly, 83 (March 1968): 40-48.

23. Padover, Saul K. "Patterns of Assassination in Occupied Territory." Public Opinion Quarterly, Winter, 1943, 680-693.

24. Paine, Lauran. The Assassins' World. New York: Taplinger, 1975.

25. Review of Reviews. "Assassins' Victims." Idem. 85 (November 1934): 15-17.

(unseen)

26. Sparrow, Gerald. The Great Assassins. New York: Arco, 1969.

27. Tischendorf, Alfred. "The Assassination of Chief Executives in Latin America." South Atlantic Quarterly, 60 (Winter 1961): 80-88.

28. Truby, J. David, and Minnery, John. Improvised Modified Firearms, V. I & V. II. Boulder: Paladin Press, 1975.

These two volumes chronicle improvised weapons from the antitank weapons to the zip gun. Given the ready availability of professionally manufactured weapons, only the disinherited terrorist might consider turning to homemade weapons of the type described. Nonetheless, the volumes are instructive as to the extent that persons have gone in the past to fabricate weapons. Extensive illustrations.

29. Truby, J. David. How Terrorists Kill: The Complete Terrorist Arsonal. Boulder:

Paladin Press, 1978.

A treatment of the implements, rather than
the mechanics of terrorism. This book is noteworthy for its 50 pages of illustrations and
photographs, most depicting weapons used by, or
suitable for use by terrorists.

30. Westermeyer, J. "Assassination in Laos: Its
    Psychosocial Dimensions." Archives of
    General Psychiatry, 28 (May 1974): 740-3.

31. Wilson, Colin. Order of Assassins: The Psy-
    chology of Murder. London: Rupert Hart-
    Davis, 1972.

2. BOMBINGS

1. Brodie, Thomas G. Bombs and Bombings: A Handbook to Detection, Disposal and Investigation for Police and Fire Departments. Springfield, IL: Charles C. Thomas, 1975.

2. Chase, L.J., ed. Bomb Threats, Bombings, and Civil Disturbances: A Guide for Facility Protection. Corvallis, Oregon: Continuing Education Publications, 1971.

3. Conference Board Record. "Terrorist Bombings Sputter Back to Normal." Idem., 10 (October 1973): 6-9.

4. Ikle, Fred C. The Social Impact of Bomb Destruction. Norman, Oklahoma: University of Oklahoma Press, 1958.

5. Lenz, Robert R. Explosives and Bomb Disposal Guide. Springfield, IL: Charles C. Thomas, 1973.

6. Mahoney, Harry T. "After a Terrorist Attack: Business as Usual." Security Management, March 1975, 16-19.

7. Pike, Earl A. Protection Against Bombs and Incendiaries: For Business, Industrial and Educational Institutions. Springfield, IL: Charles C. Thomas, 1973.

8. Stoffel, John. Explosives and Homemade Bombs. Springfield, IL: Charles C. Thomas, 1973.

9. Styles, S.G. "The Car Bomb." Journal of the Forensic Science Society, 15 (April 1975):

93-97.

10. United Nations. "Terrorist Acts Against UN
     Missions." UN Monthly Chronicle, 8 (Nov-
     ember 1971): 61-70.

11. U.S. Chamber of Commerce. Violence Against
     Society. Washington, D.C.: Idem, 1971.

12. U.S. Congress. Senate. Committee on the Ju-
     diciary. Terroristic Activity: Terrorist
     Bombings and Law Enforcement Intelligence,
     Hearings Before the Subcommittee to Inves-
     tigate the Administration of the Internal
     Security Act and Other Internal Security
     Laws, part 7. 94th Cong., 1st sess.,
     October 23, 1975.

13. _____. House. Thefts and Losses of Mili-
     tary Weapons, Ammunition, and Explosives,
     Report of the Subcommittee on Investigation
     of the Committee on Armed Services. 94th
     Cong., 2nd sess., April 14, 1976.

3. KIDNAPPING/HOSTAGE

1. Alix, Ernest Kahlar. *Ransom Kidnapping in America, 1874-1974: The Creation of a Capital Crime*. Carbondale, IL: Southern Illinois University Press, 1978.

   Terrorist ransomings receive attention *passim*.

2. *Assets Protection*, 1 (Summer 1975): entire issue.

   Devoted to "Extortion."

3. _____. "Patient Sieges: Dealing with Hostage-Takers." *Idem*. 1, no. 3 (1976): 21-27.

   Includes a recounting of cases from the U.S., Britain, Ireland and the Netherlands. Subjects treated include utility of concessions, physical containment, psychological and physical pressures, rule of mediators, and the selection, training and techniques of negotiators.

4. Baumann, Carol Elder. *The Diplomatic Kidnappings: A Revolutionary Tactic of Urban Terrorism*. The Hague: Nijhoff, 1973.

   (unseen)

5. Beall, Marshall D. "Hostage Negotiations." *Military Police Law Enforcement Journal*, 111 (Fall 1976). Reprinted in Entry A54, 223-232.

6. Blacksten, Ric and Engler, Richard. "Hostage Studies." Arlington, VA: Ketron Concept Paper, Ketron, Inc., January 8, 1974.

   (unseen)

7. Brach, Richard S. "The Inter-American Convention on the Kidnapping of Diplomats." Columbia Journal of Transnational Law, 10 (1971): 292-412.

8. Cassidy, William L. Political Kidnapping: An Introductory Overview. Boulder: Sycamore Island Books, 1978.

   An exercise in vacuousness by a security consultant. This brief (28 printed pages of large type) monograph is purported to be a sanitized "extension" from a "classified study" prepared in the summer of 1977 for a "major international police organization."

9. Clutterbuck, Richard. Kidnap and Ransom: The Response. Boston: Faber, 1978.

   Descriptions of previous incidents and prescriptions for coping.

10. _____. "Kidnapping." Army Quarterly, 104 (October 1974): 529-534.

11. Crelinston, Ronald D., and Laborge-Altmejd, Danielle, eds. Hostage Taking: Problems of Prevention and Control. Montreal: International Centre for Comparative Criminology, 1976.

    (unseen)

12. Culley, John A. "Defusing Human Bombs--Hostage Negotiations." FBI Law Enforcement Bulletin, October 1974, 10-14.

    Discussion of New York City's Hostage Negotiating Team which has been noted for its exemplary results when dealing with hostage situations.

13. Cullinane, Maurice J. "Terrorism--A New Era of Criminality." Terrorism, 1 (1978): 119-124.

In the context of the 1977 Hanafi terrorists attack in Washington, Cullinane discusses
negotiation as it functioned in that incident,
and draws conclusions that may be applicable
to future incidents. Of particular note are
his comments concerning the behavior of the
negotiator who must be chosen carefully; be
mature in appearance; never seem to be the
final authority; be able to negotiate on all
matters except the provision of weapons or
additional hostages; only respond to the demands of the terrorists, rather than attempting to be innovative; always receive a quid
pro quo; and, always keep the possibility of
escape open for the terrorists.

14. Jenkins, Brian; Johnson, Janera; and Ronfeldt,
     David. "Numbered Lives: Some Statistical
     Observations from 77 International Hostage
     Episodes". Conflict: An International
     Journal for Conflict and Policy, 1 (1978):
     71-111.

     Among the most interesting conclusions
reached by Jenkins, et. al. are the following:
the terrorist stands roughly an 80% chance of
survival in a hostage venture; the likelihood
of gaining at least some demands is roughly
50%; standard kidnapping tends to occur on the
"home turf" of the terrorists; barricade and
hostage situations are more likely to be international; American diplomats and other U.S.
representatives (official or non-official)
tend to be favorite targets, yet only in 3
incidents have explicit demands been made on
the U.S. government; no-concession policies
have not deterred, but only reshaped the act,
so that propagenda replaces concessions as the
objective; and more hostages die during assault
by anti-terrorist forces than from the direct
action of the terrorists. A very useful chronological list of annotated hostage situations
is appended.

15. Jenkins, Brian M. Hostage Survival: Some Pre-
     liminary Observations. Santa Monica, CA:
     The Rand Corp., 1976.

     The result of interviews with a number of
U.S. officials who were kidnapped and survived.

16. Jenkins, Brian M. *Terrorism and Kidnapping.* Santa Monica, Calif.: Rand Corporation, No. P-5255, June 1974.

17. Kirk, Donald. "Foiling Kidnappers." *New York Times Magazine*, February 19, 1978, 14-ff.

18. Lang, Daniel. "A Reporter at Large: the Bank Drama." *The New Yorker*, November 25, 1974, 56-126.

    On the relationships between captors and captives during the August 1973 incident at the Kreditbank, Stockholm, Sweden.

19. Lee, Andrew. "International Suppression of Hijacking." In Entry A12, 248-256.

20. McClure, Brooks. "Hostage Survival." *Conflict: An International Journal for Conflict and Policy Studies.* 1 (1978): 21-48.

    This treatment of hostage situations in the context of terrorism is a fascinating summary of many of the lessons learned from past incidents. The specialist is unlikely to find any new information, but McClure's competent synthesis should be of particular value to those whose professions might render them potential targets for terrorists, as well as those with academic interests in the dynamics of hostage survival.

21. Mickolus, Edward F. "Negotiating for Hostages: a Policy Dilemma." *Orbis*, 19 (Winter 1976): 1309-1325.

22. Miller, Abraham M. "Negotiations for Hostages: Implications from the Police Experience." *Terrorism*, 1 (1978): 125-146.

23. Miller, Judith. "Bargain with Terrorists?" *New York Times Magazine*, July 18, 1976, 7-ff.

24. Murphy, James. "The Role of International Law in the Prevention of Terrorist Kidnapping of Diplomatic Personnel." In Entry A12, 285-313.

25. Murphy, John F. "The Threat and Use of Force Against Internationally Protected Persons and Diplomatic Facilities." Paper presented to the Conference on International Terrorism, sponsored by the Ralph Bunche Institute, New York, NY, June 9-11, 1976.

26. Najmuddin, Dilshad. "Kidnapping of Diplomatic Personnel." Police Chief, February 1973, 18-23.

27. Ochberg, Frank, ed. Victims of Terrorism. Boulder, Colorado: Westview Press, 1979.

    This book centers on hostage situations, with particular attention to the victim's psychological and psychological reactions, as well as on the phenomenon of victim/terrorist alliance--the so-called Stockholm Syndrome. An annotated bibliography is included.

28. Ochberg, Frank. "The Victim of Terrorism: Psychiatric Considerations." Terrorism, 1 (1978): 147-168.

29. Pepper, Curtis B. "Kidnapped." New York Times Magazine, November 20, 1977, 42-ff.

    A factual account of an Italian kidnapping based on the fascinating chronicle of victim.

30. Platero, D. "To be Prepared Not to be Prepared." Assets Protection, 1 (1976): 16-20.

    Advice for coping with the kidnapping of loved ones.

31. Simon, Douglas W. "Policy Recommendation Exercises." International Studies Notes, 2 (Spring 1975): 19-21.

32. Souchon, Henri. "Hostage-Taking: Its Evolution and Significance." International Criminal Police Review, No. 299 (June-July 1976): 168-173.

33. Sponsler, T.H. "International Kidnapping." International Lawyer, 5 (January 1971): 25-52.

34. Stechel, Ira. "Terrorist Kidnapping of Diplo-

matic Personnel." <u>Cornell International
Law Journal</u>, 5 (Spring 1972): 189-217.

35. Stratton, J.G. "Terrorist Act of Hostage-Taking: Considerations for Law Enforcement."
<u>Journal of Police Science and Administra-
tion</u>, 6 (June 1978): 123-134.

(unseen)

36. _____. "Terrorist Act of Hostage-Taking:
A View of Violence and the Perpetrators."
<u>Journal of Police Science and Administra-
tion</u>, 6 (March 1978): 1-9.

(unseen)

37. Strentz, Thomas. "Law Enforcement Policy and
Ego Defenses of the Hostage." <u>FBI Law
Enforcement Bulletin</u>, 48 (April 1979):
2-12.

A lucid treatment of the Stockholm Syndrome
in a Freudian context. Strentz argues that the
syndrome reflects the regression of the victim
to a child-like stage of complete dependence.
Various examples of the phenomenon are offered,
as are several conditions for its coming into
play, the two most important being: the chronological length of interaction between victim
and captor, and the nature of interactions--
i.e., whether they have been positive, nega-
tive or neutral.

38. "Task Force on Kidnapping." <u>External Affairs</u>,
23 (1971): 6-11.

(unseen)

39. U.S. Congress. House. <u>Political Kidnapping,
1968-1973, A Staff Study Prepared by the
Committee on Internal Security</u>. 95th
Cong., 1st Sess., August 1, 1973.

40. Vayrnen, Raimo. "Some Aspects of Theory and
Strategy of Kidnapping." <u>Instant Research
on Peace and Violence</u>, 1 (1971): 3-21.

41. Wohlstetter, Roberta. "Kidnapping to Win
Friends and Influence People." <u>Survey</u>, 20
(Autumn 1974): 1-40.

ADDENDUM

Miron, N.S. Hostage. Kalamazoo, Michigan: Behaviordlia, Inc., 1978.

Discusses the nature of the hostage-taker, and the characteristics of an effective nego-tiator. Includes case material from U.S. hostage situations.

4. SKYJACKING

1. Aggarwala, Narinder; Fenello, Michael J.; and
   Fitzgerald, Gerald F. "Air Hijacking, An
   International Perspective." International
   Conciliation, No. 585 (November 1971):
   7-27.

   Includes treatments of political aspects
   of hijacking, and technical prevention and
   legal suppression of hijacking. An appendix
   listing the ratification states of the Tokyo,
   Hague, and Montreal Conventions is now somewhat dated; however, the overview of attempts
   to control hijacking through treatymaking is
   useful still.

2. Agrawala, S.K. Aircraft Hijacking and International Law. Dobbs Ferry, NY: Oceana,
   1973.

3. Arey, James A. The Sky Pirates. New York:
   Charles Scribner's Sons, 1971.

4. Baldwin, David A. "Bargaining with Airline Hijackers." The 50% Solution: How to Bargain Successfully with Hijackers, Strikers,
   Bosses, Oil Magnates, Arabs, Russians, and
   Other Worldly Opponents in this Modern
   World, edited by I. William Zartman. Garden City, NY: Anchor Press/Doubleday,
   1976, 404-429.

5. Barrie, G.N. "Crimes Committed Aboard Aircraft." South African Law Journal, 83
   (1968): 203-208.

6. Bell, Robert G.   "The U.S. Response to Terror-
      ism Against International Civil Aviation."
      Orbis, 19 (Winter 1976):   1326-1343.

7. Beristain, A.   "Terrorism and Aircraft Hijack-
      ing."   International Journal of Criminology
      and Penology (London) 2 (November 1974):
      347-389.

      Results of a survey of 875 persons in Mad-
      rid, and 131 university students in San Sebas-
      tian, Spain. Students (who were of Basque
      origins) were more likely to consider hijack-
      ing a political, rather than a common crime,
      when compared to the former sample.

8. Boltwood, Charles E.; Cooper, Michael R.; Fein,
      Victoria E.; and Washburn, Paul U.   "Sky-
      jacking, Airline Security, and Passenger
      Reactions: Toward a Complex Model for Pre-
      diction."   American Psychologist, 27 (June
      1972):   539-545.

      (unseen)

9. Boyle, Robert P.   "International Action to
      Combat Aircraft Hijacking."   Lawyer of the
      Americas, 4 (1972):   460-473.

      (unseen)

10. Bradford, A. Lee.   "Legal Ramifications of Hi-
      jacking Airplanes."   American Bar Associa-
      tion Journal, 48 (November 1962):   1034-
      1039.

      (unseen)

11. Brower, Charles N.   "Department Urges Senate
      Advice and Consent to Ratification of
      Montreal Convention on Aviation Sabotage."
      Department of State Bulletin, 67 (October
      16, 1972):   444-448.

12. _____.   "Aircraft Hijacking and Sabotage:
      Initiative or Inertia."   Department of
      State Bulletin, 68 (June 18, 1973):   872-
      875.

13. Chaturvedi, S.C.   "Hijacking and the Law."

Indian Journal of International Law, 11
(1971): 89-105.

(unseen)

14. Clyne, Peter. An Anatomy of Skyjacking. London: Abelard-Schuman, 1973.

15. Crelinsten, Ronald D., and Laberge-Altmejd, Danielle, eds. The Impact of Terrorism and Skyjacking on the Operation of the Criminal Justice System. Montreal: International Centre for Comparative Criminology, 1976.

16. Denero, J.M. "In-flight Crimes, the Tokyo Convention and Federal Judicial Jurisdiction." Journal of Air Law and Commerce, 35 (1969): 171-203.

(unseen)

17. Dinstein, Yoram. "Criminal Jurisdiction Over Aircraft Hijacking." Israel Law Review, 7 (1972): 195-206.

(unseen)

18. Evans, Alona E. "Aircraft Hijacking: What is to be Done." American Journal of International Law, 66 (1972): 819-822.

(unseen)

19. _____. "Aircraft Hijacking: Its Cause and Cure." American Journal of International Law, 63 (October 1969): 695-710.

20. Falk, Richard A. "The Beirut Raid and the International Law of Retaliation." American Journal of International Law, 63 (July 1969): 415-443.

21. Fenello, Michael J. "Technical Prevention of Air Piracy." International Conciliation, No. 585 (1971): 28-41.

22. Fitzgerald, G.F. "Development of International Rules Concerning Offenses and Certain Other Acts Committed on Board Aircraft." Cana-

dian Yearbook of International Law, 1
(1963): 230-251.

23. _____. "Offenses and Certain Other Acts
Committed on Board Aircraft: The Tokyo
Convention of 1963." Ibid., 2 (1964):
191-204.

24. _____. "Toward Legal Suppression of Acts
Against Civil Aviation." International
Conciliation, No. 585, (1971): 42-78.

25. Friedlander, Robert A. "Banishing Fear From
the Skies: A Statutory Proposal." Duques-
ne Law Review, 16 (1977-1978): 283-305.

26. Hawkins, G. "Skyjacking." Australian Journal
of Forensic Sciences, June 1975, 157-168.

    Includes discussion of Australian legisla-
tion.

27. Khan, Rahmatullah. "Hijacking and International Law." Africa Quarterly, 10 (1971):
398-403.

    (unseen)

28. Kolosov, Y. "Legal Questions of the Security
of Civil Aviation." International Affairs
(Moscow), April 1974, 42-46.

29. Hirsch, Arthur I., and Otis, David. "Aircraft
Piracy and Extradition." New York Law
Forum, 16 (1970): 392-419.

30. Horlick, Gary N. "The Developing Law of Air
Hijacking." Harvard International Law
Journal, 12 (1971): 33-70.

31. Hubbard, David. The Skyjacker: His Flights of
Fantasy, New York: Macmillan, 1973.

32. Israel, Ministry for Foreign Affairs. The International Civil Aviation Organization
and Arab Terrorist Organizations: A Record
of Resolutions. Jerusalem: Idem., 1973.

33. Journal of Air Law and Commerce, 37 (Spring
1971): 229-233.

Statistics on hijacking.

34. Joyner, Nancy Douglas. Aerial Hijacking as
    an International Crime. Dobbs Ferry, NY:
    Oceana, 1974.

35. Lissitzyn, Oliver J. "In-Flight Crime and U.S.
    Legislation." American Journal of Interna-
    tional Law, 67 (April 1973): 306-313.

36. Lopez Gutierrez, Juan J. "Should the Tokyo
    Convention of 1963 be Ratified?" Journal
    of Air Law and Commerce, 31 (1965): 1-21.

    (unseen)

37. McKeithen, R.L. Smith. "Prospects for the Pre-
    vention of Aircraft Hijacking Through Law."
    Columbia Journal of Transnational Law, 9
    (1970): 60-80.

    (unseen)

38. McMahon, John P. "Air Hijacking: Extradition
    as a Deterrent." Georgetown Law Journal,
    58 (1970): 1135-1152.

39. McWhinney, Edward W., et. al. The Illegal Di-
    version of Aircraft and International Law.
    Leyden: Sijthoff, 1975. Dobbs Ferry,
    NY: Oceana, 1971.

40. Mankiewicz, R.M. "The 1970 Hague Convention."
    Journal of Air Law and Commerce, 37 (1971):
    195-210.

41. Moore, Kenneth C. Airport, Aircraft and Air-
    line Security. Los Angeles: Security
    World Publishing, 1976.

42. Oren, Uri. Ninety-nine Days in Damascus: The
    Story of Professor Shlomo Samueloff and
    the Hijack of TWA Flight 840 to Damascus.
    London: Weidenfeld and Nicolson, 1970.

    A victim's account.

43. Peterson, Edward A. "Jurisdiction-Construction
    of Statute-Aircraft Piracy." Journal of
    Air Law and Commerce, 30 (1964): 292-295.

(unseen)

44. Phillips, David. Skyjack: The Story of Air
    Piracy. London: Harrap, 1973.

    Useful for its treatment of parachute-
    equipped hijackers.

45. Pulsifer, Roy, and Boyle, Robert. "The Tokyo
    Convention on Offenses and Certain Other
    Acts Committed on Board Aircraft." Journal
    of Air Law and Commerce, 20 (1964): 305-
    354.

46. Rein, Bert. "A Government Perspective."
    Journal of Air Law and Commerce, 37 (1971):
    183-193.

47. Rich, Elizabeth. Flying Scared: Why We Are
    Being Skyjacked and How to Put a Stop to
    it. New York: Stein and Day, 1972.

48. Rosenfield, Stanley B. "Air Piracy: Is it
    Time to Relax Our Security." In Criminal
    Justice Systems Review, edited by Jon S.
    Schultz and Jon P. Thomas. Buffalo: Wil-
    liam S. Hein, 1974, 67-94.

49. Shudder, Sami. "Is Hijacking of Aircraft Pir-
    acy in International Law?" British Year-
    book of International Law, 43 (1968-1969):
    193-204.

    (unseen)

50. Smith, Corin L. "Probable Necessity of an In-
    ternational Prison in Solving Aircraft Hi-
    jacking." International Lawyer, 5 (1971):
    269-278.

51. Smith, McKeithen R.N. "Prospects for the Pre-
    vention of Aircraft Hijacking Through Law."
    Columbia Journal of Transnational Law, 9
    (1970): 60-80.

    (unseen)

52. Snow, Peter and Phillips, David. The Arab Hi-
    jack War. New York: Ballantine Books,
    1970.

(unseen)

53. Steelman, H. "International Terrorism vis-a-
     vis Air Hijacking." Southwestern Univer-
     sity Law Review, 9 (1977): 85-110.

(unseen)

54. Stevenson, William. 90 Minutes at Entebbe.
     New York: Bantam Books, 1976.

55. Turner, J.S.G. "Piracy in the Air." Naval
     War College Review, 22 (1969): 86-116.

56. U.S. Congress. Senate. Committee on Finance.
     Skyjacking: Hearings on H.R. 19444. 91st
     Cong., 2nd Sess., October 6, 1970.

57. U.S. Congress. House. Committee on Interstate
     and Foreign Commerce. Aircraft Piracy,
     H.R. Report No. 91-33, 91st Cong., 1st
     Sess., 1969.

58. _____. Committee on Foreign Affairs, Sub-
     committee on Inter-American Affairs. Air
     Piracy in the Caribbean Area. 90th Cong.,
     2nd Sess., 1968.

59. U.S. Department of State. "Chronology of Hi-
     jackings--1968 through 1975." Washington,
     D.C.: 1976.

60. U.S. Department of Transportation. Federal
     Aviation Administration. Hijacking Statis-
     tics: U.S. Registered Airport, 1961-April
     1965. Washington, D.C.: 1975.

61. _____. Master List of all Hijacking At-
     tempts, Worldwide, Air Carrier, and General
     Aviation. Washington, D.C.: Office of
     Aviation Medicine, periodically updated.

62. _____. Worldwide Criminal Acts Involving
     Civil Aviation. Washington, D.C., 1975.

     Month by month summaries for 1974, includes
     data on 62 cases.

63. U.S. Federal Aviation Administration. Hijack-
     ing: Selected References, Bibliographic

List No. 18. Washington, D.C.: Idem.,
June 1969.

Over 200 annotated journalistic accounts
from 1961-1969.

64. _____. Task Force on Deterrence of Air
Piracy. Hijack Reference Data. Washington, D.C.: Idem., June 1970.

65. Van Panhuys, Harold F. "Aircraft Hijacking
and International Law." Columbia Journal
of Transnational Law, 9 (1970): 1-22.

66. Welton, Charles. Skyjack. New York: Tower,
1970.

Section H
Nuclear Terrorism and Other
Macro-Terror Possibilities

1. Albright, Joseph. Series of three articles on
   the security of nuclear weapons. Atlanta
   Journal Constitution, January 8, 15, 22,
   1978.

2. Ayers, Russell W. "Policing Plutonium: the
   Civil Liberties Fallout." Harvard Civil
   Rights/Civil Liberties Law Review, 10
   (Spring 1975): 369-443.

   The legal impact of measures which may be
   needed to prevent thefts of plutonium.

3. BDM Corporation. Analysis of the Terrorist
   Threat to the Commercial Nuclear Industry.
   Report submitted to the Special Safeguards
   Study, Nuclear Regulatory Commission of the
   U.S. Government. McLean, Virginia: Sep-
   tember 30, 1975.

   This very extensive study examines the
   skills, objectives, motivations and disincen-
   tives for nuclear terrorists considering an
   attack on civil nuclear facilities.

4. Beres, Louis Rene. "The Nuclear Threat of Terrorism." International Studies Notes (of
   the International Studies Association), 5
   (Spring 1978): 14-17.

5. _____. "Terrorism and International Security: the Nuclear Threat." Chitty's Law
   Journal, 26 (March 1978): 73-90.

   A report commissioned by the U.S. Arms
   Control and Disarmament Agency in 1977. Beres

argues that government efforts aimed at thwarting nuclear terrorism have emphasized the "technological" aspects of the problem and ignored the "behavioral" and "contextual" elements. Beres offers a description of six principal types of terrorist groups, a discussion of the considerations which will influence decision-making within the respective groups, and an extended argument for placing the problem within an international perspective. In a rather controversial proposal, Beres posits that the pattern of deterrence and reactive measures against terrorism may be complemented by a reward system. Such positive reinforcement is deemed to be especially apropos when dealing with the political terrorist who evidences a high degree of commitment (with the fedayeen being prototypical).

6. _____. "International Terrorism and World Order: The Nuclear Threat." The Stanford Journal of International Studies, XII (Spring 1977): 131-146.

Explores the factors underlying the argument that the prospect of nuclear terrorism is both credible and perilous. Beres attributes this acute threat to easy terrorist access to nuclear weapons, the contemporary changes in the terrorists "political code", and the tendency for terrorism to be condoned or at least tolerated within the international system. Beres offers three basic responses to attenuate the threat: technical fixes to render the nuclear materials less accessible, international agreements to control traffic in nuclear goods, and attempts to change the behavior of the terrorists. It is the last proposal which is the most controversial, for such attempts at behavior modification may conceivably backfire.

7. _____. "The Threat of Palestinian Nuclear Terrorism in the Middle East." International Problems, 15 (Fall 1976): 48-56.

8. _____. "Terrorism and the Nuclear Threat in the Middle East." Current History, 70 (January 1976): 27-29.

9. Berkowitz, B.J., et. al. Superviolence: the

101

Civil Threat of Mass Destruction Weapons.
Santa Barbara, Calif.:   A.D.C.O.N. Corp.,
1972.

This study by the Advanced Concept Research
Corp., includes chapters on chemical, biological and nuclear weapons.

10. Billington, George R.   "Nuclear Terrorism."
     Unpublished manuscript.   Maxwell Air Force
     Base: Air University, 1975.

11. Blair, Bruce G., and Brewer, Garry D.   "The
     Terrorist Threat to World Nuclear Pro-
     grams."   _The Journal of Conflict Resolu-
     tion_, XXI (September 1977):   379-403.

     Key contention is that the attention that
     has been focused upon the risk to commercial
     nuclear facilities has obscured a serious vul-
     nerability to the theft or unauthorized use of
     nuclear weapons by terrorists.   Many will
     quarrel with their conception of terrorism as
     a means of conflict resolution that is becoming
     increasingly attractive to "all elements of
     society".   Similarly, it is difficult to under-
     stand how nuclear terrorism is "becoming more
     practical and _legitimate_" (emphasis added).
     Several of the terror scenarios presented are
     trivial, while others are at best presented
     incompletely.   The central risk posited, that
     military officers assigned to launch facilities
     might collaborate in the arming and launching
     of Minuteman missiles grossly underestimates
     the effectiveness of existing internal security
     procedures, as well as the complexity and so-
     phistication of launch and targeting proce-
     dures.

12. Brady, David, and Rappoport, Leon.   "Policy-
     Capturing in the Field: the Nuclear Safe-
     guards Problem."   _Organizational Behavior
     and Human Performance_, 9 (April 1973).

     (unseen)

13. Burnham, David.   "Nuclear Facilities Told to
     Strengthen Antiterrorist Guard."   _The New
     York Times_, February 20, 1977, p.1.

14. California, State of.   _Nuclear Blackmail or_

Nuclear Theft Emergency Response Plan.
Sacramento: Office of Emergency Services,
1976.

A very extensive and commendable plan.
Available (microfiche copy) without charge
from: U.S. Dept. of Justice, Law Enforcement
Assistance Administration, National Criminal
Justice Reference Service, Washington, D.C.
20530. Refer to NCJ 39358 when ordering.

15. Cherico, P. "Security Requirements and Standards for Nuclear Power Plants." Security
Management, 18 (January 1975): 22-24.

16. Cohen, Bernard L. Interview by Richard Brook-
hiser. "Q & A: Understanding a Trillion-
Dollar Question." National Review, February 2, 1979, 142-155.

Cohen believes the nuclear terror possibility has been considerably overdrawn. In fact,
there are experts on terrorism who say it would
be a good thing if terrorists became preoccu-
pied with nuclear bombs, since it would dis-
tract them from more feasible methods of mass
murder.

17. _____. "The Potentialities of Terrorism:
Plutonium is an Over-rated Weapon for Ter-
rorist Use." Bulletin of the Atomic
Scientists, XXXII (June 1976): 34-35.

Cohen concludes that it is too late to engage in a dialectic concerning the utility of
nuclear power. The time for such a debate was
twenty years ago. Furthermore, he finds that
the terrorists' concern about their personal
safety would lead them to less complicated and
less dangerous mass destruction weapons--poison
gas, napalm at a sporting event, the destruction of a dam, or the poisoning of water--but
even these options are out of character with
the past activities of terrorists. Finally,
he sees yielding to terrorism as a special kind
of tyranny which society must avoid for "... to
stand fast is a guarantee of eventual victory."

18. Comey, David. "The Perfect Trojan Horse."
Bulletin of the Atomic Scientists, XXXII
(June 1976): 33-34.

Given the risk of nuclear terrorism, Comey
sees the growth of civil nuclear power programs as inimicable to civil liberties in the
U.S. Comey holds that the terrorist threat
is so severe as to "require us to alter our
traditional views about citizens' rights and
the police powers of the government." Given
the problems associated with nuclear power,
Comey would prefer to do without the "benefits"
of nuclear power rather than suffer the resultant deprivations of liberty.

19. Corporation for Public Broadcasting. "NOVA:
the Plutonium Connection." Transcript in
Congressional Record, 121 (March 11, 1975):
S3620ff.

20. Crowson, Delmar L. Progress and Prospects for
Nuclear Materials Safeguards. Vienna:
International Atomic Energy Agency, SM
133/60, 1970.

21. de Leon, Peter; Jenkins, Brian; Keller, Konrad;
and Krofcheck. Attributes of Potential
Criminal Adversaries to U.S. Nuclear Programs. Santa Monica, Calif.: Rand Corporation, R-2223-SL, February 1978. Reprinted
in: U.S. Congress, Senate, Committee on
Governmental Affairs. An Act to Combat International Terrorism, Hearings Before the
Committee on S.2236. 95th Cong., 2d sess.,
1978, 555-639.

22. DeNike, Douglas L. "Radioactive Malevolence."
Bulletin of the Atomic Scientists, February 1974, 16-20.

23. Doub, William O., and Duker, Joseph M. "Making
Nuclear Energy Safe and Secure." Foreign
Affairs, 53 (July 1975): 756-772.

24. Dror, Yehezkel. Crazy States: A Counterconven-
tional Strategic Problem. Lexington, Mass.:
Heath Lexington Books, D.C. Heath and Company, 1971.

25. Dunn, Lewis A. "Nuclear 'Gray Marketeering'."
International Security, 1 (Winter 1977):
107-118.

26. Dunn, Lewis A.; Bracken, Paul; and Smernoff,

Barry J. <u>Routes to Nuclear Weapons: As-</u>
<u>pects of Purchase or Theft.</u> Croton-on-
Hudson, N.Y.: Hudson Institute, April,
1977.

27. Edelhertz, Herbert and Walsh, Marilyn. <u>The</u>
<u>White-Collar Challenge to Nuclear Safe-</u>
<u>guards.</u> Lexington, Mass.: Lexington Books,
D.C. Heath and Company, 1978.

The authors contend that the extensive attention devoted to the nuclear terrorist threat
has overshadowed another serious threat, the
diversion of nuclear materials by employees of
the industry. This book is a competent remedy
to this largely ignored problem.

28. Epstein, William. <u>The Last Chance: Nuclear</u>
<u>Proliferation and Arms Control.</u> New York:
The Free Press, 1976.

See esp. 259-273.

29. Fine, Allan M. "Attributes of Potential Adver-
saries to U.S. Nuclear Programs." In U.S.
Department of Commerce, National Bureau of
Standards. <u>The Role of Behavioral Science</u>
<u>in Physical Security: Proceedings of the</u>
<u>Second Annual Symposium, March 23-24, 1977.</u>
Washington: 1977, 27-33.

Data indicates that the requisite combina-
tions of dedication and technical skill have
not been coextensive. "For the non-war, sub-
national, potential U.S.-based adversary, a
group possessing all the attributes of the com-
posite high-level profile would be expected to
be exceedingly rare." Fine is affiliated with
the Sandia Laboratories.

30. Flood, Michael. "Nuclear Sabotage." <u>Bulletin</u>
<u>of the Atomic Scientists</u>, XXXII (October,
1976): 29-36.

Rather than addressing illicit bomb construction, which is the wont of many commenta-
tors, Flood addresses a problem that he argues
has been neglected--the possibility that a civil
nuclear power facility might be the target of
terrorists. Of particular interest are the
tables which accompany the article, detailing

past incidents involving nuclear facilities.

31. Frank, Forrest. "Nuclear Terrorism and the Escalation of International Conflict." Naval War College Review, XXIX (Fall 1976): 12-27.

   After rehearsing the now familiar vulnerabilities that combine to create the threat of nuclear terrorism, Frank provides some interesting preliminary commentary on the possible effects that an act of nuclear terrorism might have for international relations. Proceeding from a position that views nuclear terror as an act possessed of (inherent?) ambiguity, he sees considerable risk that the act could precipitate interstate conflict. The risks range from crises resultant of retributory acts to a catalytic war.

32. Frank, Forrest R. "An International Convention Against Nuclear Theft." Bulletin of the Atomic Scientists, December 1975, p. 51.

33. _____. "Suppressing Nuclear Terrorism: A Modest Proposal." In U.S. Congress, Senate, Committee on Government Operations. Export Reorganization Act of 1976, Hearings Before the Committee on S. 1439, 94th Cong., 1st sess., June 1975, 1413-1451.

   Proposed treaty language for an international convention to suppress the theft or unlawful use of nuclear materials or weapons. The proposal is modeled after the Convention for the Suppression of Unlawful Seizure of Aircraft.

34. Fuller, John G. We Almost Lost Detroit. Pleasantville, NY: Reader's Digest Press, 1975.

   Overzealous journalism.

35. Gilinsky, Victor. "Plutonium, Proliferation and the Price of Reprocessing." Foreign Affairs, 57 (Winter 1978/1979): 374-386.

36. _____. "Diversion by National Governments." In International Safeguards and Nuclear In-

dustry, edited by Mason Willrich. Baltimore: Johns Hopkins University Press, 1973,
159-175.

37. _____. "The Military Potential of Civil
Nuclear Power." In Civil Nuclear Power and
International Security, ed. by Mason Willrich. New York: Praeger Publishers, 1971,
14-27.

Excellent background material.

38. Grant, G. M. "Physical Protection of Plants
and Materials: Physical Protection of
Special Nuclear Material in Transit." Federal Register, 39(November 13, 1974):
40036-40040.

39. Greenwood, Ted. "Discouraging Proliferation in
the Next Decade and Beyond: Non-State En-
tities." In Nuclear Proliferation: Motivations, Capabilities, and Strategies for
Control, 1980's Project of the Council on
Foreign Relations, by Ted Greenwood, Harold
A. Feiveson, and Theodore B. Taylor; New
York: McGraw-Hill Book Company, 1977,
99-107.

While Greenwood does not foreclose the possibility of terrorists aspiring to nuclear
terrorism, he does find that the most capable
groups are likely to be dissuaded by the tacit
threats of retaliation, loss of prestige, and
reprisal. Furthermore, he finds that terrorist-
inflicted casualties have been relatively limited and indeed, have been very far from the
levels of wanton human destruction that many
would associate with nuclear terrorism. His
assertion that all states share an interest in
maintaining the taboo against non-state posses-
ion of nuclear weapons may be convincing, but
could stand further development in terms of
policy implications and opportunities for diplomatic action.

40. Historical Evaluation and Research Organiza-
tion (HERO). The Terrorist and Sabotage
Threat to U.S. Nuclear Programs: Phase
One Final Report. Dunn Loring; VA: HERO,
August 1974.

(Unseen)

41.   Hutchinson, Martha C. "Defining Future Threats:
      Terrorist and Nuclear Proliferation." In
      Entry A4.

      Hutchinson's analysis of contemporary ter-
      rorism leads her to the conclusion that the harm
      done by terrorists will continue to increase
      and thus the possibility of nuclear terrorism
      is a real one. The essense of terrorism is said
      to be the willingness to accept risks in order
      to achieve political goals, such a willingness
      prevails in this analysis. In addition, Hut-
      chinson does not find that the prospect of mass
      casualities will deter at least some terrorists
      from employing nuclear weapons. Her concluding
      comments on the actions that governments may
      adopt to prevent nuclear terrorism, or failing
      that, to cope with nuclear terrorism, are likely
      to be interesting to even those who may object
      to her earlier conclusions.

42.   Imai, Ryukichi. "Nuclear Safeguards." Adelphi
      Papers, No. 86 (March 1972). London: In-
      ternational Institute for Strategic Studies,
      1972.

      An excellent primer on safeguards, and thus
      in-turn an important reference for those con-
      cerned with the technical feasibility of nuclear
      terrorism.

43.   Ingram, Timothy H. "Nuclear Hijacking: Now
      Within the Grasp of Any Bright Lunatic."
      Washington Monthly, January, 1973, 20-28.

      Popular journalism.

44.   Institute for the Study of Conflict. "Nuclear
      Power. Protest and Violence." Conflict
      Studies, 102 (December 1978).

      A useful survey of anti-nuclear movements
      in the U.S., West Germany, France, U.K., and
      Japan. A chronology of incidents is included.

45.   Jenkins, Brian M. "The Potential for Nuclear
      Terrorism." Rand P-5876. Santa Monica,
      Calif.: The Rand Corporation, May, 1977.

      While conceding the technical feasibility
      of nuclear terrorism, Jenkins argues that it

really comes down to intention, and political terrorists have never really "intended" mass murder. He dismisses organized crime as a possible nuclear terror action (due to the likely societal reaction), as he does most of the "nuts" who might find such sensational terrorism attractive, but lack the skills. The real risk is that nuclear terror may be attempted because of the adjective "nuclear", for an incident so-named will garner wide and rapt attention. Thus, nuclear terror is posited to be more attractive as a threat than as an action.

46. _____. Terrorism and the Nuclear Safeguards Issue. Santa Monica: Rand Corp., 1976.

47. _____. Will Terrorists Go Nuclear? Discuscion Paper No. 64. Santa Monica, Calif.: California Seminar on Arms Control and Foreign Policy, October 1975.

48. Karber, Phillip A., and McMengel, R.W., "A Behavioral Analysis of the Adversary Threat to the Commercial Nuclear Industry." In Entry H29.

1) "Very few groups, particularly those engaged in terrorism, have the organization, training, or level of force necessary to carry out an attack against the nuclear industry with major societal consequences." 2) Such groups which do have the resources have not operated in the U.S. 3) There are a number of non-terrorist groups that do have the resources.

49. Kelly, Orr. "If Terrorists Go After U.S. Nuclear Bombs." U.S. News and World Report, March 12, 1979, 43-45.

An informed discussion of the problem, written with more than tacit cooperation of responsible government officials.

50. Klevans, Edward M. (Film Review). American Journal of Physics, 44 (April 1976): 406-407.

Two "educational" films treating nuclear terrorism are the subject of this review. Of particular note is the "NOVA" presentation, see Entry H19.

51. Knorr, Klaus. "Is International Coercion Wan-
       ing or Rising?" International Security, I
       (Spring 1977): 92-110.

       See esp. pp. 100-102, where Knorr specu-
    lates on the great leverage that would obtain
    for the terrorist bent on international coer-
    cion based on threats of large-scale destruc-
    tion. He muses that to pay blackmail under
    such circumstances may be the lesser evil.

52. Kramer, J.J. Role of Behavioral Science in
       Physical Security: Proceedings of the
       Second Annual Symposium, March 23-24, 1977.
       Washington, D.C.: U.S. Department of Com-
       merce, National Bureau of Standards, 1978.

53. Krieger, David. "What Happens if ...? Terror-
       ists, Revolutionaries, and Nuclear Weapons."
       Annals (of the American Academy of Politi-
       cal and Social Science), 430, (March 1977),
       44-57.

       Krieger finds that the continuing expansion
    of peaceful nuclear technology will increase
    the possibility that tomorrow's terrorist will
    be armed with nuclear weapons. In addition,
    he argues the plausibility of a nuclear bomb
    being provided by a sympathetic government,
    particularly in a Middle Eastern setting. His
    description of the problems which nuclear
    armed terrorists might precipitate would rank
    such an event with history's greatest crises.

54. Kupperman, Robert H. "Facing Tomorrow's Ter-
       rorist Incident Today." A report prepared
       for the Law Enforcement Assistance Admin-
       istration, Washington, D.C. October 1977.

       This important report by the Chief Scien-
    tist of the Arms Control and Disarmament Agency,
    reviews and summarizes the results of extensive
    research funded by the Law Enforcement Assis-
    tance Administration. Kupperman takes a wide
    view of macro-terror, including nuclear, bio-
    logical and chemical options, as well as other
    significantly disruptive acts (e.g., terrorist
    interdiction of electrical grids). Special
    consideration is devoted to target hardening,
    policy choices (including cooption), incident
    management and damage limitation. An appendix

summarized several of the more impressive recent efforts at event modeling and adversary description. This report is reproduced in Entry H69.

55. Lapp, Ralph E. "The Ultimate Blackmail." New York Times Magazine, February 4, 1973, p. 13ff.

56. Larus, Joel. Nuclear Weapons Safety and the Common Defense. Columbus, Ohio. Ohio State University Press, 1967.

An early study concerned less with illicit acquisition by terrorists than with faulty control procedures.

57. Leachman, Robert B. and Althoff, Phillip, eds. Preventing Nuclear Theft: Guidelines for Industry and Government: Security Measures Conferences. NY: Praeger Publishers, 1972.

58. McPhee, John. The Curve of Binding Energy. New York: Farrar, Straus and Giroux, 1974.

Originally published as a series in The New Yorker, this is a popularized treatment of Theodore Taylor, and the possibility of the illicit fabrication of nuclear weapons.

59. Mabry, R.C. Nuclear Theft: Real and Imagined Dangers. Springfield, VA: National Technical Information Service, 1976.

(unseen)

60. Mengel, R.W. "Terrorism and New Technologies of Destruction: An Overview of the Potential Risk." In Entry A220, 443-473.

Proceeding within a costs-benefits schema, Mengel finds that terrorists--particularly in the U.S.--are not likely to assume the high risks associated with "new technology terrorism" (i.e. in particular, nuclear, chemical and biological terrorism). Alluding to--but not presenting--a data base of more than 4500 acts of terrorism, Mengel finds that terrorists are decidedly non-suicidal, that terrorists generally opt for "controllable weapons", and

111

that their activities are reducible to patterns
(a significant factor for further research).
Rejecting the "lone-individual" scenarios, it
is asserted that high technology terror is
more appropriately a (skilled) team effort.
This analysis does support the conclusion that
high technology terror could be attractive to
those wishing to escalate their efforts when
faced with likely failure at lower levels of
violence. A matrix of violent behavior is presented which distinguishes between terrorism
and seven other violent behaviors (e.g., criminal, psychopathic, etc.); however, since terrorism is never clearly defined, its utility
(i.e., the matrix) is rather questionable.
This article concludes with extended commentary
and prescription on the law enforcement and
incident-management aspects of the problem."

61.   _____. "The Impact of Nuclear Terrorism on
        the Military's Role in Society." In
        Entry A117, 402-414.

62.   MITRE Corporation. The Threat to Licensed Nu-
        clear Facilities (MTR 7022). McLean, Vir-
        ginia: September 1975.

63.   Mullen, Robert K. "Mass Destruction and Ter-
        rorism." Journal of International Affairs,
        32 (Spring/Summer 1978): 63-90.

        Probably one of the best analyses published
to date on the macro-terror problem (i.e.
nuclear, biological and chemical). Mullen
offers an informed discussion of chemical and
biological agents with mass destructive capabilities, and then proceeds to identify the
production and delivery considerations which
will affront the terrorists. His presentation
supports his conclusion that mass destruction
threats from terrorists are "vanishingly re-
mote."

64.   Nader, Ralph, and Abbotts, John. The Menace
        of Atomic Energy. New York: W.W. Norton
        & Co., Inc., 1977.

        Chapter XII, "The Plutonium Fuel Cycle,"
discusses the danger of the illicit diversion
of plutonium by terrorists and others.

65. Norman, Lloyd. "Our Nuclear Weapons Sites: Next Target of Terrorists?" Army, June, 1977, 28-31.

One of the oft-discussed routes to weapons states is the theft of an intact device. In this informative and informed article, Norman draws extensively from an interview with the Defense Department official charged with the security of nuclear weapons sites. Security procedures are outlined, as are the safety devices which preclude unauthorized use of nuclear weapons. It is conceded that a highly-skilled perpetrator might be able to disassemble and reconstruct even a weapon equipped with security devices, thus pointing up the key importance of site security.

66. Norton, Augustus R., with the assistance of Martin H. Greenberg. Understanding the Nuclear Terrorism Problem. Gaithersburg, Md.: International Association of Chiefs of Police, Inc., 1979.

A thorough examination of the nuclear terrorism problem. Although this publication is intended for senior police officials, much of it will be of wider interest. Includes a primer on the pertinent technologies, an analysis of the contending assessments of the problem, as well as an overview of the physical security and technical vulnerabilities that characterize nuclear facilities. Prospective nuclear terroists are discussed, with detailed assessments of the PLO and the F.A.L.N. The study concludes with a commentary on the implications of the nuclear terror threat--both from the aspect of practical law enforcement, and the wider implications for Constitutional protections.

67. Norton, Augustus R. "Terror by Fission: An Analysis and Critique." Chitty's Law Journal, 1979.

A critical monograph which addresses most of the literature on the nuclear terrorism question. Norton is critical of the perspective which holds that the technical feasibility of nuclear terrorism (which is itself a controversial question) demonstrates the likelihood of such an act. Instead he proposes that the motives, morals, rationality, and objectives of the terrorists must be taken into account, and that when this is done the likelihood of nuclear terrorism is at least far less than a certainty. A model of terrorists' decision-making is offered. The most important conclusion is that the terrorist groups most competent relative to an act of nuclear terror, are precisely those who would have the least to gain through such an act; the converse is also said to be true.

68. _____. "Terrorists, Atoms and the Future: Understanding the Threat." Naval War College Review, 32 (May 1979): 30-50.

A more extensive development of the arguments made in the preceding article.

69. Norton, Augustus R. and Greenberg, Martin H., eds. Studies in Nuclear Terrorism. Boston: G. K. Hall & Co., 1979.

An extensive anthology on the subject, with an original introduction by Norton. The following contributions are included: 6, 11, 17, 18, 30, 31, 39, 45, 53, 54, 60, 63, 65, 70, 71, 83, 104, 109, 110, all in this section. Robert Friedlander provides a thoughtful and incisive foreward. Indexed, with a glossary, and technical primer.

70. Norton, Augustus R. "Nuclear Terrorism and the Middle East." Military Review, LVI (April 1976), 3-11.

The Middle East is an often-mentioned setting for nuclear terrorism, with the Fedayeen (Palestinian terrorists) cited as the likely perpetrators. In this selection Norton investigates the Middle Eastern case, with particular emphasis on the acquisition of nuclear weapons, the motivation for doing so, and considerations of threat effectuation. He finds a lack of motivation among the most technically-capable Fedayeen, and a number of heretofore unrecognized problems for the terrorist bent on carrying out an act of nuclear terrorism.

71. Nuclear Energy, Policy Study Group. <u>Nuclear</u>
     <u>Power: Issues and Choices</u> (Cambridge,
     Mass.: Ballinger Publishing Company, 1977.

         See esp. pp. 301-315. While the partici-
     pants in this Ford Foundation study are con-
     cerned about inadequacies in the physical se-
     curity of nuclear reactors in the U.S. and
     abroad, they find that the difficulties in-
     volved with designing, planning,and construct-
     ing a nuclear weapon from reactor grade mat-
     erials are considerably greater than many
     experts have claimed.

72. Pendley, Robert and Scheinman, Lawrence. "In-
     ternational Safeguarding as Institutiona-
     lized Collective Behavior." <u>International</u>
     <u>Organization</u>, 29 (Summer 1975).

73. Pincus, Walter. "Scenario for a Nuclear Scare."
     <u>San Francisco Chronicle</u>, October 1, 1978.

         A report of a U.S. Department of Energy
     exercise that presumed terrorists had hidden
     a homemade atomic bomb in an urban area, and
     demanded $325 million to forestall detonation.
     Search teams reportedly found the "device" in
     less than 4 hours in 900 sq. mile area.

74. Pratt, D. Jane. "Behavior and Misbehavior of
     Terrorists: Some Cross-National Compari-
     sons."

         In Entry H29.

75. Quester, George H. "Can Proliferation Now be
     Stopped?" <u>Foreign Affairs</u>, 53, (October
     1974): 77-97.

76. Rasmussen, Norman C. "Electric Power--the
     Nuclear Option." <u>National Forum: the Phi</u>
     <u>Kappa Phi Journal,</u> 58 (Fall 1978): 13-17.

         Good terse, non-technical summary of the
     influential reactor safety study--the Rasmussen
     Report--by the primary author.

77. Rosenbaum, David M. "Nuclear Terror." <u>Inter-</u>
     <u>national Security,</u> I (Winter 1977), <u>140-</u>
     <u>161.</u>

78. Rosenbaum, David M.; Gougin, J.N.; Jefferson,
    R.M.; Kleitman, D.J.; and, Sullivan, W.C.
    Special Safeguards Study. (Washington,
    D.C.: Atomic Energy Commission, 1974).
    Excerpted in the Congressional Record,
    April 30, 1974, p. S6621.

79. Russell, Charles A.; Banker, Leon J., Jr.; and
    Miller, Bowman M. "Out-Inventing the Ter-
    rorist." Washington: U.S. Air Force
    Office of Special Investigation, n.d.

80. Salisbury, David F. "Terrorists at A-Reactors
    Called a Growing Threat." Christian
    Science Monitor, July 20, 1978, p. 9.

81. _____. "How Modern Science Prevents Nuclear
    Theft." Christ. Science Mon., 14, 7/75, 6.

82. Sanders, Benjamin. Safeguards Against Nuclear
    Proliferation. Cambridge, Mass.: MIT
    Press, 1975.

    Written for the Stockholm International
Peace Research Institute.

83. Schelling, Thomas C. "Who will Have the Bomb?"
    International Security, I (Summer 1976):
    77-91.

    Schelling's lucid article squarely addres-
ses the nuclear terrorism question as an aspect of nuclear proliferation, rather than of
political terrorism. He finds that state
actors are far more likely proliferators than
terrorists. In fact, he sees the task of
weapons construction as beyond the capability
of today's terrorists. He posits that the
Jewish terrorists of mandatory Palestine may
be prototypical for the type of organization
which would be capable of the task. His comments upon the deterrent uses to which terrorists might employ nuclear weapons are both
provocative and original.

84. Shapley, Deborah. "Plutonium: Reactor Pro-
    liferation Threatens a Nuclear Black Mar-
    ket." Science, April 9, 1971, 143-146.

    Notes several incidents of attempted or
possible thefts of nuclear materials.

85. Smith, Clifford V. "Safeguarding the Licensed Nuclear Industry." A presentation to the October 16-19, 1977, meeting of the American Nuclear Society Executive Conference on Safeguards.

   Smith is the Director of the Office of Nuclear Material Safety and Safeguards, U.S. Nuclear Regulatory Commission.

86. Smith, Roger. "Processing Plutonium: A Bitter Harvest." MBA (Master in Business Administration), March 1978, 27-29.

87. Stevenson, Adlai E. III. "Nuclear Reactors: America Must Act." Foreign Affairs, 53, (October 1974): 64-76.

88. Stanley Foundation, The. "Nuclear Theft and Terrorism: Discussion Group Report." Sixteenth Strategy for Peace Conference Report. Muscatine, Iowa: Idem., 1975.

89. Taylor, Theodore. In Statement Before Senate Committee on Governmental Affairs. 266 March 22, 1978.

   "...it is highly credible that a small group of people could design and build Fission explosives, using information and non-nuclear materials that are accessible to the public worldwide. Under some circumstances, it is quite conceivable that this could be done by one person, working alone. Such explosives could be transported by automobile. Their probable explosive yields would depend considerably on the knowledge and skills of the group. Relatively crude explosives that would be likely to yield the equivalent of up to about 1000 tons of high explosive would be much easier to build than explosives that could be reliably expected to yield the equivalent of more than 10 kilotons of high explosive. Explosives with yields in the latter range would be much easier to build with highly enriched uranium or uranium-233 than with plutonium. All three materials, including plutonium of all isotopic compositions, could be used for making relatively crude explosives with yields in the vicinity of one kiloton."

90. _____. "Commercial Nuclear Technology and Nuclear Weapon Proliferation." Nuclear Proliferation and the Near-Nuclear Countries. Edited by Onkar Marwah and Ann Schulz. Cambridge, Mass.: Ballinger Publishing Company, 1975.

A brief (13 page) selection which presents Taylor's arguments in a very accessible form.

91. Taylor, Theodore B. "Diversion by Non-Governmental Organizations." In International Safeguards and Nuclear Industry edited by Mason Willrich. Baltimore: Johns Hopkins University Press, 1973, 176-198.

92. Taylor, Theodore B., and Colligan, Douglas. "Nuclear Terrorism: A Threat of the Future?" Science Digest, August 1974, 12-17.

A popular treatment that should be readily available in community libraries.

93. Taylor, Theodore B.; Van Cleave, W.R.; Kinderman, T.M. Preliminary Survey of Non-National Nuclear Threats. Stanford: Stanford Research Institute Technical Note SSC-TN-5205-83, September, 1968.

94. U.S. Atomic Energy Commission. Environmental Survey of Transportation of Radioactive Materials to and from Nuclear Power Plants. Washington: AEC Directorate of Regulatory Standards, December 1972.

95. _____. Safeguards Research and Development: Proceedings of a Symposium, October 27-29, 1969. Springfield, VA: Clearinghouse for Federal Scientific and Technical Information, Wash. 1147, 1970.

96. _____. Physical Protection of Classified Matter and Information. (AC Manual Appendix and Revisions-2401) Washington: AEC Division of Security, June 26, 1969.

97. _____. Advisory Panel on Safeguarding Special Nuclear Material. Report to the AEC.

Washington: apparently unpublished,
March 10, 1967.

98. U.S. Comptroller-General. Improvements Needed
in the Program for the Protection of Special Nuclear Material; Report to the Congress. Washington: Government Accounting
Office, November 7, 1973.

99. U.S. Congress. Congressional Record, 122, no.
113, Staff Summary of Government Accounting
Office Report. "Shortcomings in the Systems Used to Control and Protect Highly
Dangerous Nuclear Materials--Energy Research and Development Administration."
Staff Summary. July 27, 1976.

100. _____. Senate. Committee on Government
Operations. Peaceful Nuclear Exports and
Weapons Proliferation. 94th Cong., 1st
sess., April 1975.

101. _____. House. International Relations
Committee. Nuclear Proliferation, Hear-
ings, June 8, 1976. 94th Cong., 2nd
Sess., 1976. Esp. 79-82.

102. _____. House. Small Business Committee.
Problems in the Accounting For and Safeguarding of Special Nuclear Materials,
Hearings, April 26, 1976. 94th Cong.,
2nd Sess., 1977. Esp. 111-217.

103. _____. Office of Technology Assessment.
"The Non-State Adversary." Nuclear Proliferation and Safeguards. New York:
Praeger Publishers, 1977. Chapter V.
115-136.

Prepared by the Congressional Office of
Technology Assessment, this reference proceeds
from a useful review of terrorist activities,
to a consideration of several of the non-state
adversaries that may attempt to acquire nuclear
weapons those being: the terrorist, the criminal and the mentally defective. The second
part of the section succinctly addresses the
impact that nuclear safeguards may have upon
civil liberties in the U.S., presenting syn-
opses of the three modes of confronting the
question.

104. Ward, William J. "DMSO (Dimethyl Sulfoxide):
     A New Threat in Public Figure Protection."
     Assets Protection, no. 3 (1976): 11-15.

     Minimizes the possibility that DMSO may be
     used in mixtures with poisons as an assassina-
     tion agent.

105. Willrich, Mason. "Terrorists Keep Out!"
     Bulletin of the Atomic Scientists, XXXI
     (May 1975), 12-16.

     An overview of the problem, with commentary
     on the safeguards against nuclear theft and
     sabotage taken to date, and concluding with
     recommendations for additional protective
     measures.

106. Willrich, Mason, ed. International Safeguards
     and Nuclear Industry. Baltimore: Johns
     Hopkins University Press, 1973.

     The danger of diversion and the existing
     safeguards.

107. _____. Civil Nuclear Power and Interna-
     tional Security. New York: Praeger Pub-
     lishers, 1971.

108. Willrich, Mason and Taylor, Theodore B. Nu-
     clear Theft: Risks and Safeguards.
     Cambridge, Mass.:   Ballinger Publishing
     Co., 1974.

     The influential Ford Foundation study that
     sparked much of the concerns for the prospect
     of the diversion or theft of nuclear materials
     by terrorists and criminals. Of particular
     interest is their discussion of the technology
     and the materials which might enable a few
     persons (or even one person) to construct a
     crude fission bomb or a radiological weapon.
     Their analysis of the physical security short-
     comings in the storage and shipment of nuclear
     materials is also noteworthy; however, a
     number of the deficiencies noted have since
     been corrected or ameliorated (in large part
     as a very result of their book).

109. Wohlstetter, Roberta. "Terror on a Grand
     Scale." Survival, XVIII (May/June, 1976):

98-104.

Much of the commentary and analysis of the
nuclear terrorism question is notably ahistor-
ical in emphasis, depending as it does on the
vulnerabilities resultant of modern technology.
Wohlstetter provides an anecdote to such contributions, by tracing the problem to the
earliest days of the nuclear age, and high-
lighting the developments which combine to
create the current concern. While she takes
a restrained view of the problem, she does
find cause for being disquieted, particularly
in light of contemporary examples of careless
slaughter of innocents by terrorists.

ADDENDUM

Beres, Louis Rene. Terrorism and Global Security: The Nuclear Threat. Boulder:
   Colorado: Westview Press, 1979.

Section I
United Nations

1. Bennett, W. Tapley. "U.S. Votes Against UN General Assembly Resolution Calling for Study of Terrorism." Department of State Bulletin, 68 (January 22, 1973): 81-94.

2. Bloomfield, Louis M., and Fitzgerald, Gerald F. Crimes Against Internationally Protected Persons: Prevention and Punishment (An Analysis of the UN Convention). New York: Praeger, 1975.

3. Buckley, William F., Jr. UN Journal: A Delegate's Odyssey. New York: G.P. Putnam's Sons, 1974.

   See esp. 247-252.

4. Finger, Seymour Maxwell. "International Terrorism and the United Nations." In Entry A2, 323-348.

5. Goldie, L.F.E. "Combating International Terrorism: the United Nations Developments." Naval War College Review, 31 (Winter 1979): 49-60.

6. Hoveyda, F. "The Problem of International Terrorism at the United Nations." Terrorism, 1 (1977): 71-83.

   Hoveyda, formerly permanent representative of Iran to the United Nations, reviews UN proceedings on the subject of terrorism from 1972 to the time of publication. The author argues that a "step-by-step" approach may have yielded a better result than the attempt to attain comprehensive solutions.

7. Murphy, John F. "United Nations Proposals on
    the Control and Repression of Terrorism."
    In Entry A12, 493-506.

8. United Nations. Report of the Ad Hoc Committee
    on International Terrorism. New York,
    1973.

    Covers the debate over defining terrorism,
    the causes of terrorism and measures for pre-
    vention.

9. _____. Report of the Ad Hoc Committee on
    International Terrorism. New York: 1977.

Section J
Africa (South of the Sahara)

1. Bell, J. Bowyer. "Endemic Insurgency and In-
    ternational Order: the Eritrean Exper-
    ience." Orbis, 17 (Summer 1974): 427-480.

2. Campbell, John F. "Rumblings Along the Red
    Sea: the Eritrean Question." Foreign
    Affairs, 48 (April 1970): 537-548.

3. Dortzback, Karl and Debbie. Kidnapped. New
    York: Harper and Row, 1975.

    Memoirs of a missionary who was kidnapped
    in 1974 by the Eritrean Liberation Front. Some
    of the names have been changed to protect the
    guilty.

4. Fanon, Franz. Towards the African Revolution:
    Political Essays trans. by Haakon Cheva-
    lier. New York: Grove, 1967.

5. Felt, Edward. Urban Revolt in South Africa,
    1960-1964: A Case Study. Evanston, IL:
    Northwestern University Press, 1971.

6. Gibson, Richard. African Liberation Movements:
    Contemporary Struggles Against White Min-
    ority Rule. New York: Oxford University
    Press, 1972.

7. Hempstone, I. Rebels, Mercenaries, and Divi-
    dends: the Katanga Story. New York:
    Praeger, 1962.

8. Horrell, Muriel. Terrorism in Southern Africa.
    Johannesburg: South African Institute of
    Race Relations, 1968.

9. Jacobs, W.D., and Yarborough, W.P. Terrorism in Southern Africa: Portents and Prospects. New York: American African Affairs Association, Inc., 1973.

   Treats groups in South Africa, Rhodesia, Namibia, Angola and Mozambique.

10. Mojekwu, Christopher. "From Protest to Terror. Violence: the African Experience." In Entry A117, 177-181.

11. Morris, Michael. Armed Conflict in Southern Africa: A Survey of Regional Terrorism From Their Beginnings to the Present, with a Comprehensive Examination of the Portuguese Position. Cape Town, South Africa: Jeremy Spence, 1974.

    Includes useful case material, maps and bibliographies for groups active since 1950 in Rhodesia, Mozambique, Angola, Portuguese Guinea, Zambia, Tanzania, Malawi, South-west Africa, South Africa, and Botswana.

12. _____. Terrorism. Cape Town: Howard Timmins, 1971.

13. South African Institute of Race Relations. Security and Related Trials in South Africa, July 1976-May 1977. Johannesburg: 1977.

14. _____. Administration of Security Legislation in South Africa, January 1976-March 1977. Johannesburg: 1977.

15. Sundiata, I.K. "Integrative and Disintegrative Terror: the Case of Equatorial Guinea." In Entry A117, 182-194.

16. Teixeira, Bernardo. The Fabric of Terror. New York: The Derin-Adair Company, 1965.

    Written by a Portuguese, this book chronicles a particularly gruesome spate of anti-colonial terrorism which occurred in Angola during March 1961. Whatever the impetus for this book, it was definitely not intended for the faint of heart. Eight pages of gory photographs have been included.

17. Venter, Al J. *Africa at War*. Old Greenwich, Conn: Devin-Adair, 1974.

18. _____. *The Terror Fighters*. Cape Town and Johannesburg: Purnell, 1969.

ADDENDUM

Efrat, Edgar S. "Terrorism in South Africa." In Entry A2, 194-208.

Section K
Asia

1. Azad, Abul Kalam. India Wins Freedom. Calcutta: Orient Longmans, 1959.

2. Bains, Chester A. Vietnam: The Roots of Conflict. Englewood Cliffs, NJ: Prentice-Hall, 1967.

3. Burki, S.J. "Social and Economic Determinants of Political Violence: A Case Study of the Punjab." Middle East Journal, 25 (1971): 465-480.

4. Crozier, Brian. South-East Asia in Turmoil. Baltimore: Penguin, 1965.

5. Hosmer, Stephen T. Viet Cong Repression and Its Implications for the Future. Lexington, Mass.: Heath Lexington Books, 1970.

6. Kuriyama, Yoshihiro. "Terrorism at Tel Aviv Airport and a 'New Left' Group in Japan." Asian Survey, 13 (March 1973): 336-346.

    Focuses upon the emergence of the United Red Army, as well as its tactics and ideology.

7. Lambrick, H.T, trans. The Terrorist. London: Ernest Benn, Ltd., 1972.

    Unseen, but apparently deals with the Sind region of present-day Pakistan during the last years of the British colonial period.

8. Mallin, Jay. Terror in Viet Nam. Princeton: D. Van Nostrand, 1966.

9. Matsushita, T. <u>Youthful Extremism in Japan</u>.
    Tokyo: United Nations, Asia and Far East
    Institute for the Prevention of Crime and
    Treatment of Offenders, 1977.

    A brief (8 pp.) report dealing with the
    trends in extremist activities by Japanese
    students, the causes of such extremism, and
    criminal sanctions appropriate to the problem.

10. O'Ballance, Edgar. <u>The Indo-China War, 1945-
    1954: A Study in Guerrilla Warfare</u>. Lon-
    don: Faber and Faber, 1964.

11. _____. <u>The Red Army of China</u>. London:
    Faber and Faber, 1962.

12. Pike, Douglas. <u>The Viet-Cong Strategy of
    Terror</u>. Saigon: U.S. Mission, 1970.

13. Pye, Lucian W. <u>Guerrilla Communism in Malaya:
    It's Social and Political Meaning</u>. Prince-
    ton: Princeton University Press, 1956.

14. Qureshi, Saleem. "Political Violence in the
    South Asian Subcontinent." In Entry A2,
    151-193.

15. Rhan, M.A. <u>Guerrilla Warfare: Its Past, Pre-
    sent and Future</u>. Karachi, India: Rangrut,
    1960.

16. Singh, Khushwant, and Singh, Satindra. <u>Ghadar
    1915: India's First Armed Revolution</u>.
    New Delhi: R.K. Publishing House, 1966.

17. Steinhoff, Patricia. "Portrait of a Terrorist:
    An Interview with Kozo Okamoto." <u>Asian
    Survey</u>, 16 (September 1976): 830-845.

18. Taylor, Robert W., and Byong-Suh Kim. "Vio-
    lence and Change in Postindustrial Socie-
    ties: Student Protest in America and Japan
    in the 1960's." In Entry A117, 204-219.

19. U.S. State Department. <u>A Study: Viet Cong Use
    of Terror</u>. Saigon: U.S. Mission in Viet-
    nam, 1967.

20. Valeriano, Napoleon D., and Bohannon, Charles
    T.R. Counterguerrilla Operations: The
    Phillippine Experience. New York: Prae-
    ger, 1966.

ADDENDUM

Pike, Douglas. Viet Cong: The Organization
    and Techniques of the National Liberation
    Front of South Vietnam. Cambridge: The
    M.I.T. Press, 1966.

Section L
Latin America

1. Alsina, Geronimo. "The War and the Tupamaros." *Bulletin Tricontinental*, August 1972, 29-42.

2. Alves, M.M. "Kidnapped Diplomats: Greek Tragedy on a Latin Stage." *Commonweal*, 92 (1970): 311-14.

3. _____. *A Grain of Mustard Seed*. Garden City, NY: Doubleday Anchor Press, 1973.

4. Andreski, Stanislav. *Parasitism and Subversion: The Case of Latin America*. New York: Pantheon, 1967.

5. Bejar, Hector. *Peru 1965: Notes on a Guerrilla Experience*. Translated by William Rose. New York: Monthly Review, 1970.

6. Blackburn, Robin, ed. *Strategy for Revolution: Essays on Latin America by Regis Debray* (New York: Monthly Review, 1970).

7. Booth, John A. "Rural Violence in Columbia, 1948-1963." *Western Political Quarterly*, 27, December, 1974, 657-679.

8. Callahan, Edward F. "Terror in Venezuela." *Military Review*, 49 (1969): 49-56.

9. Chaplin, David. "Peru's Postponed Revolution." *World Politics*, 20 (April 1968).

10. Cobo, Juan. "The Roots of 'Violencia'." <u>New Times</u>, (August 5, 1970), 25-27.

11. Connolly, Stephen and Druehl, Gregory. "The Tupamaros: The New Focus in Latin America," <u>Journal of Contemporary Revolutions</u>, 3, No. 3 (Summer 1971): 59-68.

12. Costa-Gavras and Solinas, Franco. <u>State of Siege</u>. (Trans. of Screenplay by Brooke Leveque). New York: Ballantine, 1973.

13. Craig, Alexander. "The Urban Guerrilla in Latin America." <u>Survey</u>, 17, Summer, 1971, 112-128.

14. Davis, Jack. <u>Political Violence in Latin America</u>. London: International Institute for Strategic Studies, 1972.

15. Deakin, Thomas J. "The Legacy of Carlos Marighella." <u>FBI Law Enforcement Bulletin</u>, 43, No. 10 (October 1974): 9-15.

16. Debray, Regis. <u>Revolution in the Revolution?: Armed Struggle and Political Struggle in Latin America</u>. (Trans. by Bobbye Ortiz) New York: Monthly Review Press, 1967.

    This brief book has had considerable influence in leftist circles in Latin America and elsewhere. It is strongest on tactics for mobilizing the guerrilla potential of the urban and rural masses.

17. D'Oliviera, Col. S.L. "Uruguay and the Tupamaro Myth." <u>Military Review</u>, 53, No. 4 (April 1973).

18. Duff, Ernest A., and McCamant, John F. <u>Violence and Repression in Latin America: A Quantitative and Historical Analysis</u> (Riverside, New Jersey: Free Press, 1975).

19. Einaudi, Luigi R. "Latin American Student Radicalism: A Different Type of Struggle." (Santa Monica: The Rand Corporation, P-3897, July 1968), 16 pp.

20. Evans, Robert D. <u>Brazil, the Road Back From</u>

Terrorism. Montreal: McGill-Queen's University Press, 1975.

21. Foland, Frances M. "Uruguay's Urban Guerrillas: A New Model for Revolution?" New Leader, 54, October 4, 1971, 8-11.

22. Gadea, Hilda. Ernesto: A Memoir of Che Guevara. Garden City, NY: Doubleday, 1972.

23. Gerassi, John, ed. Venceremos: The Speeches and Writing of Che Guevara (London: Panther, 1968): 606 pp.

24. Gerassi, Maria. "Uruguay's Urban Guerrillas." New Left Review (London), 62, July-August, 1970, 22-29.

25. Gilio, M.E. The Tupamaro Guerrillas. New York: Ballantine, 1970.

26. _____. The Tupamaro Guerrillas. Trans. by Anne Edmondston and with an Introduction by Robert J. Alexander. New York: Saturday Review Press, 1972.

27. Gott, Richard. Guerrilla Movements in Latin America. London: Thomas Nelson and Sons Ltd., 1970.

    Basically a survey of guerrilla movements, Gott provides excellent coverage of activities in Guatemala, Venezuela, Columbia, Peru, and Bolivia. Eleven appendices provide additional information.

28. Guillen, Abraham. Philosophy of the Urban Guerrilla. Trans. and edited by Donald C. Hodges. New York: Morrow, 1973.

29. Halperin, Ernst. Terrorism in Latin America. The Washington Papers, No. 38. Beverly Hills: Sage Publications, 1976.

30. Hernandez, Julion. "The Tupamaros Attack a Garrison: A Step-by-Step Account." In

James Kohl and John Litt, <u>Urban Guerrilla</u>
<u>Warfare in Latin America</u>." Cambridge,
Mass.: The MIT Press, 1974.

Cuban news service text of an account of
an attack on the Uruguayan Navy Training
Center. One of the best accounts of its type,
rich in detail, and thoroughly absorbing.

31. Horowitz, Irving Louis; de Castro, Jose; and
Gerassi, John, eds. <u>Latin American Radica-</u>
<u>lism 1969</u> (London: Johnathan Cape, 1969),
656 pp.

32. Huberman, Leo; and Sweezy, Paul M., eds. <u>Re-</u>
<u>gis Debray and the Latin American Revolu-</u>
<u>tion</u> (New York: Monthly Review Press,
1968): 330 pp.

33. Jackson, Sir Geoffrey. <u>Surviving the Long</u>
<u>Night: An Autobiographical Account of a</u>
<u>Political Kidnapping</u>. New York: The Van-
guard Press, 1974.

A restrained, yet fascinating account of
244 days in a Tupamaro captivity by the former
British Ambassador to Uruguay. Particularly
noteworthy are Jackson's descriptions of his
environment and the terrorists with whom he
came into contact. The sophistication of the
Tupamaros in conducting surveillance, abduct-
ing their victim, maintaining his incarceration
and releasing him is to be contrasted to the
naive and short sighted political perspectives
espoused by Jackson's captors. Surprisingly, there was rather more compassion--
with notable exceptions--among the Ambassador's
captors than one might have expected. On another level, <u>Surviving the Long Night</u> is an
often inspiring account of how one man coped
with a most extraordinary experience.

34. James, Daniel, ed. <u>The Complete Bolivian Di-</u>
<u>aries of Che Guevara and Other Captured</u>
<u>Documents</u> (New York: Stein and Day, 1968):
330 pp.

35. Janke, Peter. "Terrorism in Argentina." <u>RUSI</u>
<u>Journal for Defense Studies</u>, 119 (Septem-
ber 1974): 43-44.

36. Jaquett, S.J. "Women in Revolutionary Move-
    ments in Latin America." Journal of Mar-
    riage and the Family (May 1973): 344-354.

37. Johnson, Kenneth F. "Guatemala: From Terror-
    ism to Terror." Conflict Studies, No. 23,
    (May 1972).

38. _____. Guerrilla Politics in Argentina.
    London: Institute for the Study of Con-
    flict, 1975.

39. Johnson, Kenneth L. "On the Guatemalan Poli-
    tical Violence." Politics and Society
    (4:1), Fall, 1973, 55-82.

40. Kohl, James and Litt, John (eds.). Urban
    Guerrilla Warfare in Latin America. Cam-
    bridge, Mass.: The MIT Press, 1974.

    An excellent collection of essays and in-
    terviews with urban terrorists from Brazil,
    Uruguay, and Argentina. The book also con-
    tains a useful bibliography.

41. Larteguy, Jean. The Guerrillas. (Trans. by
    Stanley Hochman) New York: World Pub-
    lishing Company, 1970.

    Useful as a survey of guerrilla movements
    in Latin America. Terrorist activities per
    se receive little attention.

42. Litt, John and Kohl, James. "The Guerrillas
    of Montevideo." The Nation, 214, Febru-
    ary 28, 1972, 269-272.

43. Marighella, Carlos. "Questions of Organiza-
    tion." In James Kohl and John Litt, Urban
    Guerrilla Warfare in Latin America. Cam-
    bridge, Mass.: The MIT Press, 1974.

    A classic radical statement by one of the
    leading revolutionaries in Brazil. It lists
    major "rules" of behavior for those engaged
    in terrorist or guerrilla activity.

44. Martirena, Luis. "How the Tupamaros Attacked
    the Homes of Four Uruguayan Police Offici-
    als." In James Kohl and John Litt, Urban

Guerrilla Warfare in Latin America. Cambridge, Mass.: The MIT Press, 1974.

A brief account of the tactics employed.

45. Max, Alphonse. Tupamaros: A Pattern for Urban Guerrilla Warfare in Latin America. The Hague: International Documentation and Information Centre, 1970.

46. Mercier Vega, Luis. Guerrillas in Latin America: The Technique of the Counter-State. (Trans. by Daniel Weissbort) London: Pall Mall Press, 1969.

This book contains a brief history of the guerrilla, several short theoretical chapters, and a survey of the "National Situation" in Venezuela, Argentina, Columbia, Guatemala, Bolivia, Brazil, Paraguay, and Peru at the time of writing. Its usefulness is limited by a lack of depth.

47. Moss, Robert. "Urban Guerrillas in Uruguay." Problems of Communism, 20, September, 1971, 14-23.

48. Nunez, Carlos. The Tupamaros. New York: Times Change Press, 1970.

49. Porzicanski, A.C. Uruguay's Tupamaros: The Urban Guerrilla. New York: Praeger, 1973.

50. Quartim, Joao. "Leninism or Militarism?" In James Kohl and John Litt, Urban Guerrilla Warfare in Latin America. Cambridge, Mass.: The MIT Press, 1974.

Quartim, a former leader of the Brazilian VPR, addresses the question of the effects of guerrilla and terrorist activity on the goals and morals of a movement.

51. Russell, Charles A., and Robert E. Hildner. "Urban Insurgency in Latin America: Its Implications for the Future." Air University Review, 22, No. 6 (1971): 55-64.

52. Sinclair, Andrew. Guevara. London: William Collins and Sons, 1970.

53. Suarez, Hector Victor. "The Revolutionary
     Armed Forces: With Che's Weapons." In
     James Kohl and John Litt, Urban Guerrilla
     Warfare in Latin America. Cambridge,
     Mass.: The MIT Press, 1974.

     A brief account of Argentinian (FAR) think-
     ing on the question of urban guerrilla warfare.

54. Tischendorf, Alfred. "The Assassination of
     Chief Executives in Latin America." South
     Atlantic Quarterly, 60, No. 1 (Winter 1961):
     80-88.

55. Truskier, A. "Politics of Violence: The Urban
     Guerrilla in Brazil: Interview with Four
     Revolutionists." Ramparts Magazine, 9,
     October, 1970, 30-34.

     Interesting interview with four leading
     Brazilian guerrilla leaders: Angelo Pezzutti,
     Carlos Eduardo Fleury, Ladislaw Dobor, and
     Fernando Nagle Gabeira.

56. Wilson, Carlos. Tupamaros: The Unmentionables.
     Boston: Branden Press, 1974.

     By an insider, who has provided primary
     materials (communiques, transcripts, etc.) and
     an apologia for the Tupamaros as well as a
     diatribe against the U.S. government and its
     role in Uruguay.

Section M
Middle East and North Africa

1.   Adie, W.A.C. "China, Israel and the Arabs."
     Conflict Studies, No. 12 (May 1971).

2.   Aines, Ronald C. "The Jewish Underground
     Against the British Mandate in Palestine."
     M.A. Thesis, Union College, 1973.

     (unseen, but cited in several authoritative
     works)

3.   Alexander, Yonah. "From Terrorism to War:
     The Anatomy of the Birth of Israel." In
     Entry A2.

4.   _____. "Terrorism and the Media in the
     Middle East." In Entry A4.

5.   Antonius, George. The Arab Awakening. Beirut:
     Khayat, 1955.

6.   Al-Ayouty, Yassin. "Egypt and the Palestini-
     ans." Current History, January 1973,
     5-12, 39.

7.   _____. "Palestinians and the Fourth Arab-
     Israeli War." Current History, February
     1974, 74-78.

8.   Arafat, Yasser. Address to the 29th Session of
     the United Nationa General Assembly, Nov-
     ember 13, 1974. New York Times, November
     14, 1974.

9.   Austria. Federal Chancellery. The Events of
     September 28 and 29, 1973: A Documentary
     Report. Vienna: idem, 1973.

10. Avner (pseud.). _Memoirs of an Assassin_, trans.
    by Burgo Partridge. New York: Thomas
    Yoseloff, 1959.

    An account by a member of the Irgun.

11. Bauer, Yehuda. _From Diplomacy to Resistance:_
    A History of Jewish Palestine, 1939-1945.
    Philadelphia: Jewish Publication Society,
    1970.

    (unseen)

12. Begin, Menachem. _The Revolt._ Revised ed.
    New York: Dell Publishing Co., Inc., 1977.

    The complete text of the 1952 edition with
    addition of a brief preface (2 pages) written
    in 1977, and a 10 page preface written in 1972.
    Clearly one of the best auto-biographical ac-
    counts of a terrorist campaign available. Per-
    haps no other book better illustrates the
    off-repeated dictum--"one man's freedom fight-
    er is another man's terrorist." Begin's
    omissions are frequently as revealing as his
    text.

13. Bell, J. Bowyer. "Arafat's Man in the Mirror:
    The Myth of the Fedayeen." _New Middle_
    East (London) 19 (April 1970): 19-24.

14. _____. _Terror Out of Zion: Irgun Zuai_
    Leumi, LEHI, and the Palestine Underground,
    _1929-1949._ New York: St. Martin's Press,
    1977.

    A very ample chronicle of terrorism in man-
    datory Palestine. Extensive attention is
    directed to the Irgun Zuai Leumi and Lehamey
    Heruth Israel (LEHI--popularly known as the
    Stern Gang). Bell's Treatment is clearly the
    best descriptive work on the subject in English,
    although a more explicit analytical focus would
    have enhanced its value. A brief bibliogra-
    phic section is noteworthy, as are the numerous
    photographs produced throughout the book.

15. Ben-Porat, Yeshayahu; Haber, Eitani and Schiff,
    Zeev. _Entebbe Rescue._ New York: Dela-
    courte Press, 1977.

138

Entebbe Rescue is reportedly the "official"
Israeli version of the daring operation. Notable especially for the key role ascribed to
Shimon Peres, Minister of Defense at the time
of the rescue.

16. Borisov, J. Palestinian Underground: The
    Story of Jewish Resistance. New York:
    Judea Publishing Co., 1947.

17. Borodin, Nikolai. "The Palestinian Resistance
    Movement: A Soviet View." New Middle East
    (London), December 1972, 27-28.

    A Soviet response to the Munich incident.

18. Brandon, Henry. "Jordan: The Forgotten Cri-
    sis (1): Were We Masterful..." Foreign
    Policy, No. 10 (Spring 1973): 158-170.

19. Calvert, Peter. "The Diminishing Returns of
    Political Violence." New Middle East (Lon-
    don), May 1973, 25-27.

20. Chaliand, Gerard. The Palestinian Resistance.
    Middlesex: Penguin, 1972.

21. Clark, Michael K. Algeria in Turmoil. New
    York: Praeger, 1959.

22. Cohen, Guela. Women of Violence: Memoirs of
    a Young Terrorist, 1943-1948, trans. by
    Hillel Halkin. New York: Holt, Rinehart,
    and Winston, 1966.

23. Cohen, M.J. "British Strategy and the Pales-
    tine Question." Journal of Contemporary
    History 7, Nos. 3-4 (July-October 1972).

24. Colebrook, Joan. "Israel--With Terrorists."
    Commentary, July 1974, 30-39.

25. Cooley, John K. "Moscow Faces a Palestinian
    Dilemma." Mid East 11 (1970): 32-35.

26. _____. "China and the Palestinians."
    Journal of Palestine Studies, V. 1, No. 2,
    (1972), 19-34.

27. _____. Green March, Black September. (Lon-
    don: Frank Cass and Company Ltd., 1973)

Effective chapters on Arafat, Habash and other Fedayeen leaders. Cooley is the highly respected, former Middle East correspondent for the Christian Science Monitor. He writes from a perspective sympathetic to the Palestinians (vis-a-vis the Fedayeen).

28. Curtis, Michael; Meyer, Joseph; Waxman, Chaim I.; and Pollack, Allen. The Palestinians: People, History, Politics. New Brunswick, NJ: Transaction Books, 1975.

A collection of previously published materials, many by Israelis.

29. DeKel, Ephraim (pseud. Krasner). Shai: Historical Exploits of Haganah Intelligence. New York: Yoseloff, 1959.

30. Dershowitz, Alan M. "Terrorism and Preventive Detention: The Case of Israel." A Commentary Report (1970): 3-14.

(unseen)

31. Dinstein, Yoram. "Terrorism and War of Liberation: An Israeli Perspective of the Arab-Israeli Conflict." In Entry A12, 155-172.

32. Dobson, Christopher. Black September: Its Short, Violent History. New York: Macmillan, 1974.

Popular history with a surfeit of gratuitous ethnocentric and partisan commentary. Dobson's assertion of the Arab's "fatal flow of violence" is illustrative. He argues that Black September operated under al-Fatah auspices, although the facts would seem to indicate a cooperative relationship. Despite several significant errors, the book contains material of note with respect to Black September. In particular, the identification of Black September principals, as well as an account of the Israeli-Fedayeen "secret war" should be of interest. Dobson is a journalist with the British Sunday Telegraph.

33. Ellenberg, Edward S. "The PLO and its Place
    in Violence and Terror." In Entry A117,
    165-176.

34. Fallaci, Oriana. "A Leader of Fedayeen: 'We
    Want a War Like the Vietnam War': Inter-
    view with George Habash." Life, June 12,
    1970, 32-34.

35. Fishman, Gideon. "Criminological Aspects of
    International Terrorism: The Synamics of
    the Palestinian Movement." In Marc Riedel
    and Terence P. Thornberry, eds. Crime and
    Delinquency: Dimensions of Deviance. New
    York: Praeger, 1974, 103-113.

    (unseen)

36. Foley, Charles, and Scobie, W.I. The Struggle
    for Cyprus. Stanford: Hoover Institution
    Press, 1975.

37. Franjeck, S. "How Revolutionary is the Pales-
    tinian Resistance: A Marxist Interpreta-
    tion." Journal of Palestine Studies 1
    (1972): 52-60.

38. Frank, Gerald. The Deed. New York: Simon
    and Schuster, 1963.

    An account of Lord Moyne's assassination
    by a reporter who covered the trial of the
    assassins.

39. _____. "The Moyne Case: A Tragic History."
    Commentary, December 1945, 64-71.

40. Freedman, Robert O. "Soviet Policy Toward In-
    ternational Terrorism." In Entry A2,
    115-147.

41. Gitlin, Jan. Conquest of Acre Prison. Tel
    Aviv: Hardar, 1962.

42. Great Britain. H.M. Stationery Office. Ter-
    rorism in Cyprus: The Captured Documents.
    Trans. extracts issued by authority of the
    Secretary of State for the Colonies. 1956.

43. Grivas-Dighenes, General George. Guerrilla

Warfare and EOKA's Struggle--A Politico-Military Study, trans. by A.A. Pallis. London: Longmans, 1964.

An important treatment by the leader of the National Organization of Cypriot Fighters (EOKA).

44. Groussard, Serge. The Blood of Israel: The Massacre of the Israeli Athletes, the Olympics, 1972, trans. by Harold J. Salemson. New York: Morrow, 1975.

(unseen, but reportedly strong on the negotiations between the terrorists and German authorities.)

45. Hamid, Rashid. "What is the PLO?" Journal of Palestinian Studies, V. 4 (Summer 1975): 90-109.

Basic summary of the organizational development of the PLO. A useful chronological piece, including a chart on p. 102 showing the organizational structure, but no names.

46. Harkabi, Y. "Fedayeen. Action and Arab Strategy." Adelphi Paper, No. 53, December 1968. The Institute for Strategic Studies, 18 Adam Street, London.

47. Heikal, Muhammed M. The Road to Ramadan. New York: Quadrangle, 1975.

The Fedayeen, passim.

48. Henissart, Paul. Wolves in the City. New York: Simon and Schuster, 1970.

An extensive history of the OAS.

49. Heradstveit, Daniel. "A Profile of the Palestine Guerrillas." Cooperation and Conflict 7 (1972): 13-36.

(unseen)

50. Heradstveit, David. "The Role of International Terrorism in the Middle East Conflict and its Implications for Conflict Resolu-

tion." In David Carlton and Carlo Schaerf, eds. International Terrorism and World Security. New York: The Halstead Press, 1975, 93-103.

51. Holden, David. "Which Arafat?" New York Times Magazine, March 23, 1975, 11ff.

52. Horvitz, J.F. "Arab Terrorism and International Aviation: Deterrence Versus the Political Act." Chitty's Law Journal, 24 (May 1976): 145-154.

53. Howley, Dennis C. The UN and the Palestinians. New York: Exposition, 1975.

54. Hudson, Michael C. "The Palestinian Arab Resistance Movement: Its Significance in the Middle East Crisis." Middle East Journal, 23 (1969): 291-301.

55. _____. "Developments and Setbacks in the Palestinian Resistance Movement." Journal of Palestine Studies, 1 (Spring 1972): 64-84.

56. _____. "The Palestinian Factor in the Lebanese Civil War." Middle East Journal, 32 (Summer 1978): 261-278.

    Discusses the fragmentation of the Fedayeen into three main tendencies: pro-Syrian, middle of the road, and rejectionist.

57. Hurewitz, Jacob C. The Struggle for Palestine. New York: Greenwood, 1968.

58. Hussain, Mehmood. The Palestine Liberation Organization: A Study in Ideology and Tactics. New York: International Publications Service, 1975.

59. Hutchinson, Martha C. Revolutionary Terrorism: The FLN in Algeria, 1954-1962. Stanford, Calif.: Hoover Institution Press, 1978.

    A study of the use of terrorism by the FLN. Hutchinson identifies several functions for terrorism including compliance, endorsement, disorientation, isolation and organizational.

143

Concludes that the FLN "victory" in Algeria
was less a case of the terrorists "winning"
than it was of a government "losing". She sees
the confluence of a number of fortuitous factors producing the victory, and she asserts
that terrorism as the "unique means of resistance" can only succeed in "rare circumstances."
The book should be read with a competent history of the conflict (e.g., Alistair Horne's
A Savage War of Peace).

60. Institute for the Study of Conflict. "Since
    Jordan: The Palestinian Fedayeen." Con-
    flict Studies, No. 38 (September 1973).

61. Israel. Nasser Terror Gangs: The Story of
    the Fedayeen. Jerusalem: Ministry for
    Foreign Affairs, 1956.

62. _____. "Accessories to Terror: The Res-
    ponsibility of Arab Governments for the Or-
    ganizations of Terrorist Activities."
    Middle East Information Series. Jerusalem:
    Ministry for Foreign Affairs, Division of
    Information, Israel Information Centre,
    July, 1973.

    1968-1973 chronology of Arab terrorist
    activities, with information on Arab govern-
    mental aid to terrorist groups.

63. Jabber, Fuad. "The Arab Regimes and the Pales-
    tinian Revolution, 1967-1971." Journal
    of Palestine Studies, 2 (Winter 1973):
    79-101.

64. Joiner, Charles. The Fedayeen and Arab World
    Politics. Morristown, NJ: General Learn-
    ing Press, 1974.

65. Kadi, Leila S., ed. Basic Political Documents
    of the Armed Palestinian Resistance Move-
    ment. Beirut: Palestine Liberation Or-
    ganization Research Center, 1969.

66. Katz, Doris. The Lady was a Terrorist: During
    Israel's War of Liberation, Intro. by Kon-
    rad Bercovici. New York: Shiloni, 1953.

67. Katz, Samuel. Days of Fire: The Secret His-

tory of the Irgun Zuai Leumi. Garden City,
NY: Doubleday, 1968.

68. Kiernan, Thomas. Arafat: The Man and the
    Myth. New York: Norton, 1976.

69. Kimche, Jon. "Can Israel Contain the Palestine
    Revolution?" Conflict Studies, No. 13
    (June 1971).

70. _____. "Israel and the Palestinians."
    In The Arab-Israeli Dispute. London: In-
    stitute for the Study of Conflict, 1971.

71. Kuroda, Yasumasa. "Young Palestinian Comman-
    dos in Political Socialization Perspective."
    Middle East Journal 26 (Summer 1972):
    253-70.

72. Laffin, John. Fedayeen: The Arab-Israeli
    Dilemma (New York: The Free Press, 1973).

        Pro-Israeli, though the author alleges that
    he has written a fair account. The theme of
    the work is that the fedayeen really do not re-
    present the Palestinian people, but only them-
    selves. Laffin portrays a movement splintered,
    that would best serve the Palestinians by dis-
    appearing. "But, this will not happen. Re-
    sistance has become an industry; the fedayeen
    organizations have become entrenched bureau-
    cracies in which the hierarchy are reluctant
    to eliminate their own authority."

73. Lewis, Bernard. "The Palestinians and the
    PLO: A Historical Approach." Commentary,
    January 1975, 32-48.

74. Little, Thomas. "New Arab Extremists: A View
    From the Arab World." Conflict Studies, 4
    (May 1970).

75. _____. "The Nature of the Palestinian Resis-
    tance Movement." Asian Affairs, 57 (1970):
    159-169.

76. McIntyre, Ronald R. "The Palestine Liberation
    Organization: Tactics, Strategies and Op-
    tions Toward the Geneva Peace Conference."
    Journal of Palestine Studies, IV, (Summer

145

1975): 65-89.

77. Mallison, W.T., Jr., and Mallison, S.V. "An
     International Law Appraisal of the Juri-
     dicial Characteristics of the Resistance
     of the People of Palestine: The Struggle
     for Human Rights." In Entry A12, 173-190.

78. Mardor, Munya. Haganah. New York: New Amer-
     ican Library, 1966.

     (unseen)

79. Medzini, Roni. "China and the Palestinians."
     New Middle East (London), No. 32, 34-40.

80. Meridor, Yaacov. Long is the Road to Freedom.
     Johannesburg: Newzo Press, 1955.

     By Begin's predecessor in the Irgun.

81. Moughrabi, Fouad. "The Refusal Front: A Study
     of the High Risk Politics in the Palestine
     Resistance Movement." Paper presented to
     the International Studies Association,
     Toronto, Canada, February 25-29, 1976.

82. Muslih, Muhammad Y. "Moderates and Rejection-
     ists Within the Palestine Liberation Organ-
     ization." Middle East Journal, V. 30
     (Spring, 1976): 127-140.

83. Nakleh, Emile A. "The Anatomy of Violence:
     Theoretical Reflections on Palestinian Re-
     sistance." Middle East Journal, 25
     (Spring 1971): 180-200.

84. Norden, Eric. "The Politics of Death." Pent-
     house, August 1973, 52ff.

85. Norton, Augustus R. Moscow and the Palestin-
     ians. Miami: Center for Advanced Interna-
     tional Studies, University of Miami, 1974.

     Traces the evolving relationship through
     the summer of 1974, with special emphasis upon
     the Soviet perspective.

86. _____. "The Palestinian State Under PLO
     Leadership." A paper presented at the

April 1976 annual meeting of the Mid-West
Political Science Association, Chicago,
Illinois.

An examination of the "aura of responsibility thesis" which holds that a revolutionary
movement, once established in a state, will
turn inward to the tasks of development and
administration, and away from terrorism and
violence.

87. O'Ballance, Edgar. "Some Arab Guerrilla Prob-
    lems." Military Review, 52 (October 1973):
    27-34.

88. _____. Arab Guerrilla Power, 1967-1972.
    Hamden, Conn.: Archon Books, 1973.

A competent journalistic treatise by an
author who has written extensively about conflict in the Middle East, inter alia.

89. O'Neill, Bard E. Revolutionary Warfare in the
    Middle East: The Israelis versus the Fed-
    ayeen. Boulder, Colorado: Paladin, 1974.

90. _____. "Towards a Typology of Political
    Terrorism: The Palestinian Resistance
    Movement." Journal of International Af-
    fairs, 32 (Spring/Summer 1978): 17-42.

91. O'Neill, Major Bard E. (USAF). "Israel and
    the Fedayeen: Persistance or Transforma-
    tion." Strategic Review, V.IV, (Spring
    1976): 89-101.

The article is a faint cry for Israeli-
Palestinian talks aimed at the emergence of
a mini-state, based on guarantees, provisions
for Israeli sanctions, a moderate PLO government, no purge of non-Fedayeen, and joint economic ties, as well as the continued existence
of Jordan.

92. Palestine Liberation Organization. The "Acti-
    vities" of the Hagana, Irgun and Stern
    Bands. New York: idem, n.d.

(unseen)

93. Paust, J.J. "Selected Terroristic Claims Arising from the Arab-Israeli Conflict." Akron Law Review, 7 (Spring 1978): 404-421.

94. Peretz, Don. "Arab Palestine: Phoenix or Phantom?" Foreign Affairs, 48 (January 1970): 322-333.

95. Politics in Uniform: A Study of the Military in the Arab World and Israel compiled by An-Nahar Arab Report Research Staff. London: Cooperative Printing Company, S.A.L., 1972.

    Pp. 75-88 treat the PLO.

96. Pryce-Jones, David. The Face of Defeat: Palestinian Refugees and Guerrillas. New York: Holt, Rinehart, and Winston, 1972.

97. Quandt, William B.; Jabber, Fuad; and Lesch, Ann M. The Politics of Palestinian Nationalism. Berkeley: University of California Press, 1973.

    Still the best work on the Fedayeen.

98. Rapoport, David. "The Politics of Atrocity." In Entry A4, 46-61.

99. Rapoport, S.E. "Between Minimal Courage and Maximum Cowardice: A Legal Analysis of the Release of Abu Daoud." Brooklyn Journal of International Law, 3 (Spring 1977): 195-209.

100. al-Rayyes, Riad, and Nahas, Dunia. Guerrillas for Palestine. New York: St. Martin's Press, 1976.

    A balanced and concise primer on the Fedayeen. Of particular note are sections dealing with the political apparatus within the PLO (and especially summaries of each National Assembly session through the 12th of 1974); Fedayeen relations with the Arab states and the U.S.S.R. and P.R.C.; and profiles of the principal leaders. On the negative side the book lacks any analysis of Fedayeen ideological po-

148

sitioning, or any treatment of terrorism _per
se_.

101. Romaniecki, Leon. The Arab Terrorists in the
     Middle East and the Soviet Union. Jeru-
     salem: Soviet and East Europeon Research
     Center, Hebrew University of Jerusalem,
     1973.

102. Schiff, Zeev, and Rothstein, Raphael. Feday-
     een: Guerrillas Against Israel. New York:
     McKay, 1972.

103. Schmidt, Dana A. Armageddon in the Middle East.
     New York: John Day, 1974.

     See especially pp. 114-193 treating the
     Palestinian guerrillas.

104. Sharabi, Misham. Palestine Guerrillas: Their
     Credibility and Effectiveness. Washington:
     Center for Strategic and International
     Studies, Georgetown University, 1970.

105. _____. "Liberation or Settlement: The
     Dialectics of Palestinian Struggle." Jour-
     nal of Palestine Studies, II, (Winter
     1973): 33-48.

     "The Palestinian experience has tended to
     develop largely independently of systematic
     theory, which, as expressed in institutions
     and behavior, lagged behind. Theory and rhe-
     toric were indistinguishable, and practice
     mostly took one form of spontaneous, disorgan-
     ized activity."

106. Sheehan, Edward R.F. "Why Sadat and Faisal
     Chose Arafat." New York Times Magazine,
     December 8, 1974, 31ff.

     The article proposes that Sadat engineered
     the split in the Palestinian resistance move-
     ment by having Arafat espouse the acceptance
     of a limited state.

107. Slater, Leonard. The Pledge. New York: Simon
     and Schuster, 1970.

     (unseen, but reportedly worthwhile for the

author's chronicle of the arming of the Haganah.

108. Sobel, Lester A., ed. Palestinian Impasse:
      Arab Guerrillas and International Terror.
      New York: Facts on File, Inc., 1977.

      A very handy reference work.

109. (Soviet Union). "The Soviet Attitude to the
      Palestine Problem." Journal of Palestine
      Studies, 2 (Autumn 1972): 187-212.

      An important document (believed to be legi-
      timate), comprising a critique of the political
      program of the Syrian Communist Party by So-
      viet officials (asserted to be Mikhail Suslov
      and Boris Ponomarev). Included in the exten-
      sive commentary are arguments against "adven-
      turism" and "extremism" (basically to be
      understood as counter-productive violence
      vis-a-vis "revolutionary violence.")

110. Stetler, Russell, ed. Palestine: The Arab-
      Israeli Conflict. Palo Alto, Calif.:
      Ramparts Press, 1974.

      (unseen)

111. Tinnin, David B. Hit Team. Boston: Little,
      Brown, 1976.

      (unseen)

112. U.S. Congress. House. International Rela-
      tions Committee. Palestinian Issue in
      Middle East Peace Efforts, Hearings Before
      Special Subcommittee on Investigations,
      September 30, 1975. 94th Cong., 1st
      Sess., 1976.

113. U.S. Congress. Senate. Foreign Relations
      Committee. Terrorist Attack at Istanbul
      Airport, Senate Report 94-1235, September
      16, 1976. 94th Cong., 2nd Sess., 1976.

114. Weisband, Edward, and Roguly, Damir. "Pales-
      tinian Terrorism: Violence, Verbal Stra-
      tegy and Legitimacy." In Entry A2, 258-
      319.

115. Wiener Library Bulletin. "Scope and Limit of
     a Fedayeen Consensus." Idem., (1970/1971):
     1-8.

116. Wilson, R.D. Cordon and Search. Aldershot:
     Gale and Polden, 1949.

     A British view of terrorism in mandatory
     Palestine.

117. Wolf, John B. "Black September: Militant Pa-
     lestinianism." Current History, January,
     1973, 5-8, and 37.

118. Yodfat, Aryeh. "The Soviet Union and the Pa-
     lestine Guerrillas." Mizan, January/Feb-
     ruary 1969, 8-17. (See Soviet Union Sup-
     port of Fedayeen File)

     Good piece, especially on Soviet criticism
     of the Fedayeen's tactics. ". . . a paradox-
     ical situation developed: The Soviet Union
     was supporting a movement and its activities
     not because it liked them, but because it felt
     it would gain too much unpopularity by opposing
     them, whereas support would entitle it to a
     certain measure of supervision."

Section N
North America

1. Beaton, Leonard. "Crisis in Quebec." Round
   Table, 241, 1971, 147-152.

2. Bordenkircher, D.E. "Prisons and the Revolutionary." Prepared for the American Correctional Association, Annual Congress of
   Correction, 104th Proceedings, Houston,
   Texas, August 18-22. 1974. College Park,
   Md.: American Correctional Association,
   1975.

3. Broehl, Wayne G. The Molly Maquires. Cambridge: Harvard University Press, 1974.

4. Brown, Richard M. Strain of Violence: His-
   torical Studies of American Violence and
   Vigilantism. London: Oxford University
   Press, 1975.

5. Chalmers, D.M. Hooded Americanism. New York:
   Quadrangle, 1968

6. Cleaver, Eldridge. Soul on Ice. New York:
   Dell Publishing Co., 1968.

7. Daniels, Stuart. "The Weathermen." Government
   and Opposition, 9 (Autumn 1974): 430-459.

8. Dawson, Henry B. The Sons of Liberty. New
   York: 1859.

   (unseen)

9. Deakin, Thomas J. "The Legacy of Carlos Marighella." FBI Law Enforcement Bulletin, 43
   (October 1974): 19-25.

Relates Marighella's Minimanual to the activities of U.S. groups (Weathermen, Black
Panthers, and the SLA).

10. Fainstein, N.I., and Fainstein, S.S. Urban
     Political Movements: The Search for Power
     by Minority Groups in American Cities.
     Englewood Cliffs, NJ: Prentice Hall, 1974.

11. Foner, P.S. Black Panthers Speak. Philadel-
     phia: J.B. Lippincott, 1970.

     Collection of statements and essays.

12. Gellner, John. Bayonets in the Streets: Urban
     Guerrillas at Home and Abroad. Don Mills,
     Ontario: Collier-Macmillan, 1974.

     Includes a careful examination of the
     events of 1970 in Canada.

13. Goode, Stephen. Affluent Revolutionaries: A
     Portrait of the New Left. New York: New
     Viewpoints, Franklin Watts, 1974.

     A useful account of the New Left, with the
     emphasis upon the U.S.

14. Green, L.C. "Terrorism--the Canadian Exper-
     ience." In Entry A2, 3-29.

15. Holt, Simma. Terrorism in the Name of God:
     The Story of the Sons of Freedom Doukho-
     bors. NY: Crown Publishers, 1965.

16. Jacobs, Harold, ed. Weatherman. New York:
     Ramparts Press, 1970.

     A very useful collection of original ma-
     terials by the entire panoply of student ac-
     tivists, and radical leftists. A number of
     official Weatherman documents are included
     (26 of some 50 selections).

17. Jay, Martin. "Politics of Terror." Partisan
     Review, 38 (1971): 95-103.

     A not unsympathetic critique of the terror
     of the New Left. Jay holds that the New Left
     terrorists have wrought destruction without any

153

ideological sense of what they were "making"
in the process. The posits that one of the
explanations for the shift to action (vis-a-
vis) words is the very freedom of expression
which has decreased the "power of words"; thus
we find the New Left seeking more demonstrative
tactics.

18. Johnpoll, Bernard. "Terrorism and the Mass
     Media in the United States." In Entry
     A4, 157-165.

19. _____. "Perspectives on Political Terrorism
     in the United States." In Entry A2, 30-
     45.

20. (Kahane, Meir)."Meir Kahane: A Candid Conversa-
     tion with the Militant Leader of the
     Jewish Defense League." Playboy, October
     1972, 69ff.

21. Lerner, M. "Anarchism and the American Counter-
     culture." Government and Opposition, 5
     (1970): 430-455.

22. Lipset, Seymour M., and Rabb, Earl. The Poli-
     tics of Unreason, 2nd edition. Chicago:
     University of Chicago Press, 1978.

23. Miller, Michael J., and Gilmore, Susan. Revo-
     lution at Berkley. New York: Dial, 1975.

24. Morf, Gustave. Terror in Quebec: Case Studies
     of the FLQ. Toronto: Clarke, Irvin and
     Company, 1970.

     Written by a psychologist, this book is es-
pecially noteworthy for the report of the findings of hundreds of interviews with incarcera-
ted members of the FLQ.

25. Moore, Brian. The Revolution Script. New York:
     Holt, Rinehart and Winston, 1971.

     A popular account of the Cross and LaPorte
kidnappings by the Quebec Liberation Front.

26. Morris, Robert. "Patty Hearst & the New Ter-
     ror." New Republic, November 22, 1975,
     8-10.

27. Mosbey, J.C. Prison--Terrorist Link. Bessemer, Alabama: Cerberus, Inc., Criminal Justice Consultants, 1977.

28. O'Brion, Leon. Dublin Castle and the 1916 Rising. New York: New York University Press, 1971.

29. Pearsall, R.B., ed. Symbionese Liberation Army: Documents and Communications. Amsterdam: Rudopi N.V., Keizergracht, 1974.

30. Popov, M.I. "American Extreme Left: A Decade of Conflict." Conflict Studies, 29 (December 1972).

31. Redlick, Amy S. "Transnational Factors Affecting Quebec Separatist Terrorist." Paper presented at the annual convention of the International Studies Association, Toronto, Canada, February 25-29, 1976.

32. Reichert, William D. Partisans of Freedom: A Study in American Anarchism. Bowling Green: Bowling Green University Popular Press, 1976.

33. Regush, Nicholas M. Pierre Vallieres: The Revolutionary Process in Quebec. New York: Dial, 1973.

    (unseen)

34. Revel, Jean-Francois. Without Marx or Jesus: The New American Revolution has Begun. Garden City, NY: Doubleday & Co., 1971.

35. Sale, Kirkpatrick. SDS. New York: Random House, 1973.

36. Saywell, John. Quebec 70: A Documentary Narrative. Toronto: University of Toronto Press, 1971.

37. Schultz, D. Subversive. Springfield, IL: Charles C. Thomas, 1973.

    Characteristics and goals of the Black Panthers, White Panthers, U.S. Communist Party, SDS, Black Muslims, and others.

38. Sears, D.D., and McConahay, J.B. Politics of Violence: The New Urban Blacks and the Watts Riot. Boston: Houghton Mifflin, 1973.

39. Stewart, James. The FLQ: Years of Terrorism. Richmond Hill: Montreal Star, 1970.

    Journalistic account by a newspaperman.

40. U.S. Comptroller General. U.S. General Accounting Office. FBI Domestic Intelligence Operations: Their Purpose and Scope: Issues that Need to be Resolved. Washington, D.C. 1976.

    An extensive report which calls for legislation to clarify the purpose and scope of FBI domestic intelligence operations. Conclusions based upon the study of 797 randomly sampled cases from 1974.

41. U.S. Congress. House. Committee on Internal Security. America's Maoists--The Revolutionary Union--The Venceremos Organization--Report by the Committee. Washington, D.C., 1972.

42. _____. Revolutionary Activities Directed Toward the Administration of Penal or Correctional Systems, Parts 1-4, Hearings. 93rd Cong., 1st Sess., March 29; May 1; June 25; July 12, 14, 25, 1973.

43. _____. Political Kidnappings, 1968-1973: A Staff Study. 93rd Cong., 1st Sess., Washington, D.C. August 1, 1973.

    Includes case material on 35 incidents and summary treatments of the 16 terrorist groups responsible.

44. _____. Revolutionary Target: The American Penal System, House Report 93-738. 93rd Cong., 1st Sess., December 18, 1973.

45. _____. The Symbionese Liberation Army, Committee Print. 93rd Cong., 2nd Sess., February 18, 1974.

46. _____. Domestic Intelligence Operations for

Internal Security Purposes, Part 1,
Hearings. 93rd Cong., 2nd Sess., February
20, April 1,2,8; June 4,5, 1974.

47. _____. Terrorism. Hearings Before the
Committee, Part 1. February 27-28,
March 21-22, 26, 1974. 93rd Cong., 2nd
Sess., Washington, D.C., 1974.

48. _____. Terrorism, Hearings Before the Committee on Internal Security. 93rd Cong.,
2nd Sess., February through August, 1974.

Parts I-IV - Summary of each part.

49. _____. The Workers World Party and Its
Front Organizations Hearings, 93rd Cong.,
2nd Sess., April 1974.

50. _____. Terrorism and Hearings Before the
Committee, Part 2, May 8,14,16,22,29,30,
June 13, 1974, 93rd Cong., 2nd Sess.,
Washington, D.C., 1974.

51. _____. Terrorism. Hearings Before the
Committee, Part 3. June 26-27, July 10-11,
23, August 13, 1974. 93rd Cong., 2nd Sess.,
Washington, D.C., 1974.

52. _____. Terrorism, Hearings Before the Committee. Part 4, July 30, August 1,15,20,
1974. 93rd Cong., 2nd Sess., Washington,
D.C., 1974.

53. _____. Terrorism: A Staff Study. Prepared by the Committee on Internal Security.
93rd Cong., 2nd Sess., August 1, 1974.

54. _____. Committee on the Judiciary. FBI
Counter-Intelligence Programs, Hearings
Before the House Civil Rights and Consti-
tutional Rights Sub-committee, November 20,
1974. 93rd Cong., 2nd Sess., Washington,
D.C., 1974.

55. U.S. Congress. Senate. Terroristic Activity,
Part 2: Inside the Weatherman Movement,
Hearings Before the Sub-committee on In-
ternal Security. 93rd Cong., 2nd Sess.,
October 24, 1974.

56. _____. Terroristic Activity: Hostage Defense Measures, Hearings Before the Subcommittee to Investigate the Administration of the Internal Security Act and Other Internal Security Laws, Part 5. 94th Cong., 1st Sess., July 25, 1975.

57. _____. Judiciary Committee. Terroristic Activity, Part 6: The Cuban Connection in Puerto Rico; Castro's Hand in Puerto Rico and U.S. Terrorism, Hearings Before the Sub-committee on Internal Security. 94th Cong., 1st Sess., July 30, 1975.

58. _____. Nationwide Drive Against Law Enforcement Intelligence Operations, Hearings Before the Senate Subcommittee to Investigate the Administration of the Internal Security Act and Other Internal Security Laws, September 18, 1975. Washington, D.C., 1975.

59. _____. Revolutionary Activities Within the U.S.: The American Indian Movement, Hearings Before the Subcommittee on Internal Security, April 6, 1976. 94th Cong., 2nd Sess., 1976.

60. _____. Terroristic Activity: Terrorism in the Miami Area, Part 8, Hearings Before the Subcommittee on Internal Security, May 6, 1976. 94th Cong., 2nd Sess., 1976.

    Includes interview with a former anti-Castro terrorist.

61. _____. Nationwide Drive Against Law Enforcement Intelligence Operations, Hearings Before the Subcommittee on Internal Security, September 1976, 94th Cong., 1st Sess., 1976.

62. _____. Judiciary Committee. Revolutionary Activities Within the U.S. The American Indian Movement. Committee Print. 94th Cong., 2nd Sess., September, 1976.

ADDENDUM

DeLeon, David. The American as Anarchist: Re-

158

flections on Indigenous Radicalism. Baltimore: Johns Hopkins Univ. Press, 1978.

Draws a picture of native American radicalism as a distinct variety of political ideals,
standing opposed to European manifestations of
radicalism.

Maurer, Marvin. "The Ku Klux Klan and the National Liberation Front: Terrorism Applied
to Achieve Diverse Goals." In Livingston
(Section A), 131-152.

McLellan, Vin, and Avery, Paul. Voices of Guns.
NY: G.P. Putnam's Sons, 1977.

Unseen, but reportedly a thorough account
of the SLA.

Section O
Western Europe

1. Agirre, Julen. <u>Operation Orgo: The Execution</u>
    <u>of Admiral Luis Carrero Blanco.</u> Trans. by
    Barbara P. Solomon. New York: Quadrangle
    Books, 1975.

2. Baumann, Michael. <u>Terror or Love?</u> <u>Bommi Bau-</u>
    <u>mann's Own Story of His Life as a West</u>
    <u>German Urban Guerrilla.</u> New York: Grove
    Press, Inc., 1979. (Reprint of 1977 edi-
    tion published by the Pulp Press, Inc.)

    Translation of <u>Wie alles anfing</u> which
    was banned in the Federal Republic. One of the
    rare first-person accounts by a German terror-
    ist. Baumann was an early member of the June
    2nd Movement, and the Wieland Commune. Unfor-
    tunately his rambling--even incoherent--account
    sheds little light on the broader questions
    raised by the left's resort to terrorism in
    Germany. If anything, the book seems to be
    prototypical of the confusion and alienation
    that describes many of those associated with
    the violence of the Left. A useful chronology.

3. Becker, Jillian. <u>Hitler's Children: The Story</u>
    <u>of the Baader-Meinhof Terrorist Gang.</u>
    Philadelphia: Lippincott, 1977.

    Although the title is problematic, <u>Hitler's</u>
    <u>Children</u> is the most thorough account of the
    West German terrorists available. While
    Becker is less than systematic, the informa-
    tion she provides on terrorist activities is
    both interesting and useful. On the whole she
    weaves a story of terrorists cum-criminals who
    could claim upper-middle class backgrounds, at

least some university education and a basic
contempt for authority. It is also interesting to note the degree to which the central
members shared disruptive familial backgrounds.
In contrast to the notion that terrorists are
systematic, efficient and dedicated to their
tasks, Becker's terrorists often lack purpose,
political objectives or an organizing intellectual framework or ideology. Key instances
of ineptitudes are also illuminating. Becker
also provides an essential who's who of West
German terrorists (7 pp.).

4. Beckett, J.C. "Northern Ireland." Journal of
        Contemporary History, 6 (1971): 121-134.

5. Bell, J. Bowyer. "Strategy, Tactics, and Ter-
        ror: An Irish Perspective." In Entry A2,
        65-89.

6. _____. "Violence and Italian Politics."
        Conflict: An International Journal for
        Conflict and Policy Studies. 1 (1978):
        49-69.

        Bell sees the violence of the last decade
in Italy as a reflection of the inability of
the political system to accomodate dissent.
To buttress his argument he points not only to
the activism of the extreme right and left,
but also to the "Neo-Luddites" of Northern
Italy who have engaged in violence and destruction not out of ideological impetuses, but
from the frustration and discontent produced
by the system. His portrait of the intricate
web of conspiracy, provocation, violence and
counter-violence involving the left and the
right is nicely done, although he clearly un-
derestimates the potential of several of the
groups (esp. Brigate Rosse, in light of the
Moro murder--which occured after the article
was written). He makes much of the payment
of $800,000 (U.S.) to General Miceli who was
later implicated in the abortive coup of 1970,
but here he leaves the reader with a matter
which could probably stand further scholarly
investigation.

7. _____. "The Escalation of Insurgency: The
        Experience of the Provisional IRA (1969-
        1971)." The Review of Politics, 35 (July

1973): 398-411.

8. _____. "The Chroniclers of Violence in
Northern Ireland: The First Wave Interpre-
ted." The Review of Politics, 34 (October
1974): 521-543.

9. _____. The Secret Army: A History of the
IRA. London: Anthony Blond; Cambridge:
MIT Press, 1974.

10. Bennett, Richard L. The Blacks and the Tans.
Boston: Houghton Mifflin, 1959.

11. Birrell, Derek. "Relative Deprivation as a
Factor in the Conflict in Northern Ireland."
Sociological Review, 20 (August 1972):
317-343.

12. Boulton, David. The Ulster Volunteer Force,
1966-1973: An Anatomy of Loyalist Rebellion. Dublin: Gill and MacMillan, Torc
Books, 1973.

13. Bowden, Tom. "The IRA (Irish Republican Army)
and the Changing Tactics of Terrorism."
Political Quarterly, 47 (October/December
1976): 425-437.

14. Boyle, K. and Hillyard, P. Law and State:
The Case of Northern Ireland. London:
Martin Robertson and Company, Ltd., 1975.

15. Bradshaw, Jon. "The Dream of Terror." Es-
quire, July 18, 1978, 24-50.

16. Burnett, H.B., Jr. "Interview with Sean Mc
Bride." Skeptic, January/February 1974,
8-11, and 54-57.

McBride was former leader of the IRA.

17. Carr, Gordon. The Angry Brigade: A History
of Britain's First Urban Guerrilla Group.
London: Gollancz, 1975.

18. Chambard, Claude. The Marquis: A History of
the French Resistance Movement. Indiana-

polis: Bobbs-Merrill, 1976.

19. Clissold, Stephen, ed. A Short History of Yu-
     goslavia: From Early Times to 1966. Cam-
     bridge: Cambridge University Press, 1966.

     Some material on the Croatian terrorists
can be found in this book.

20. Clutterbuck, Richard. "Intimidation of Wit-
     nesses and Juries." Army Quarterly, 104
     (April 1974): 285-294.

21. Coogan, Tim Pat. The IRA: New York: Praeger,
     1970.

22. Council of Europe. European Convention on the
     Suppression of Terrorism. Strasbourg,
     France, 1977.

     The 16 articles of the convention treat
extradition, disputes, jurisdiction and types
of terrorist offenses. Should be used with:
"Explanatory Report on the European Convention
on the Suppression of Terrorism" (Strasbourg,
1977).

23. Crozier, Brian, ed. New Dimensions of Security
     in Europe. London: Institute for the
     Study of Conflict, May 1975.

24. Crozier, Brian. Ulster: Politics and Terror-
     ism. London: Institute for the Study of
     Conflict, 1973.

     This pamphlet surveys the causes and the
issues involved in the Northern Ireland situation. An appendix provides some useful material on the militant terrorist wings of the
Protestants and the Catholics.

25. Economist. "Anarcho-Nihilism." Idem. 237,
     no. 6635, 1970, 2-33.

26. Elliott, John D. "Action and Reaction: West
     Germany and the Baader-Meinhof Guerrillas."
     Strategic Review, 4 (Winter 1976): 60-67.

27. Elwin, G. "Swedish Anti-Terrorist Legislation."
     Contemporary Crises (Amsterdam), 1 (July

1977): 289-301.

Describes and critiques the Emergency Anti-
terrorist Law passed in Sweden in 1973. Key
civil liberties deficiency is the notion of the
"presumptive terrorist" (vis-a-vis the proven
terrorist).

28. Gleason, J. Bloody Sunday. London: Davies,
1962.

The IRA terrorism that contributed to the
founding of the Free State.

29. Goodhart, Philip. The Climate of Collapse:
The Terrorist Threat to Britain and Her
Allies. Petersham, Surrey: Foreign Af-
fairs Publishing Co., Ltd., June 1975).

A conservative member of Parliament argues
for a firm policy against terrorists, in contrast to the permissive policy being carried
out by the British government.

30. Goodman, R.W., Jr.; Hoffman, J.E.; McClanahan,
J.R.; and Tompkins, T.C. "Compendium of
European Theater Terrorist Groups." Maxwell Air Force Base, Ala.: Air University,
1976.

Compendium includes groups active in Cyprus,
Germany, France, Greece, Iran, Italy, Netherlands, Portugal, Spain, Turkey, UK and the
Middle East. Each chapter includes a bibliography.

31. Great Britain. Report of the Commission to
Consider Legal Procedures to Deal with Ter-
rorist Activities in Northern Ireland.
London, 1972.

32. Hachey, Thomas E. "Political Terrorism: The
British Experience." In Entry A2, 90-114.

33. Hamilton, Iain. "The Irish Tangle." Conflict
Studies, 6 (1970).

34. Horchem, Hans J. "West Germany's Red Army
Anarchists." Conflict Studies, 46 (June
1974).

Horchem concludes that the Rote Armee Frak-
tion (Baader-Meinhof Gang) was engaged in anarchistic conflict, despite its activists' claims
to the contrary. In contrast to international
terrorism, the domestic terrorism of the RAF
is unlikely to succeed--although it will not
die out either. This overview is noteworthy
for its references to terrorists' documents in
German, many of which are not readily available
in English.

35. _____. "Right Wing Extremism in Western
        Germany." Conflict Studies, 65 (1975).

36. _____. "The Urban Guerrilla in West Ger-
        many--Origins and Perspectives." Unpub-
        lished paper presented at the U.S. Depart-
        ment of State Conference on Terrorism,
        Washington, D.C., March 25-26, 1976.

37. Howard, A.J. "Urban Guerrilla Warfare in a
        Democratic Society." Medicine, Science and
        the Law (Bristol, England), 12 (October
        1972): 231-243.

        The implications of terrorism in Northern
Ireland for the forensic scientist.

38. IRA. Handbook for Volunteers of the Irish Re-
        publican Army. Issued by IRA General
        Headquarters, 1965.

39. Janke, Peter, and Price, D.L. "Ulster: Con-
        sensus and Coercion." Conflict Studies,
        50 (1974).

40. Jenkins, Roy. England: Prevention of Terror-
        ism. (Temporary Provisions)--A Bill.
        London: Her Majesty's Stationery Office,
        1974.

41. Korsch, Karl. Marxism and Philosophy. London:
        NLB, 1970. New York: Monthly Review
        Press, 1971.

        Said to be one of the gospels of the stu-
dent movement in West Germany.

42. Lasky, Melvin J. "Ulrike Meinhof and the
        Baader-Meinhof Gang." Encounter, 44 (June

1975): 9-23.

43. _____. "Ulrike and Andreas: The Bonnie
and Clyde of West Germany's Radical Sub-
culture May Have Failed to Make a Revolution, but They Have Bruised the Body Poli-
tic." New York Times Magazine, May 11,
1975, 14ff.

44. Lowry, D. "Ill Treatment, Brutality and Tor-
ture: Some Thoughts Upon the 'Treatment'
of Irish Political Prisoners." DePaul
Law Review, 22 (1973): 553ff.

45. MacStiofain, Sean (pseud.) Revolutionary in
Ireland. Farnborough, UK: Gordon Cre-
monesi, 1975.

    Apparently the autobiography of the Chief
of Staff of the Provisional IRA, John Edward
Drayton Stephenson. Stephenson was largely
responsible for the split between the Provos
and the officials. As expected, he argues the
case for violence as a political tool.

46. McGuire, Maria. To Take Arms: My Years With
the IRA Provisionals. New York: Viking,
1973.

47. Martino, Antonio. "Making Democracy Unsafe
for Italy." The American Spectator, June/
July 1978, 15-16.

    This University of Naples economics profes-
sor and official in the Italian Liberal Party,
argues that a symbiotic relationship (at least)
exists between the Brigate Rosse and the Italian Communist Party, in that the actions of
the terrorists enable the PCI to assert its
identification with the political establishment
and the concomitant necessity that it be included in any national government.

48. Merritt, Richard L. "From Munich to Mogadishu."
The American Spectator, June/July 1978,
17-19.

    Addressing the possibility of an authori-
tarian reaction by the West German government
to the terrorist exploits of the Red Army

Faction, inter alia, Merritt finds the danger
lies not in what has occured to date, but what
might develop in the future. Summarizing the
legal and administrative steps that have been
taken to dampen the terrorist threat, he argues that pressure from the right may result
in measures which will place "state security
above personal freedoms," and thus play into
the hands of the terrorists. The most significant problem is said to arise from the super-
heated political environment, resultant of terrorism, which precludes rational debate and
consequently could lead to a breakdown in political consensus.

49. Moss, Robert, and Hamilton, Iain. "The Spread-
ing Irish Conflict." Conflict Studies, 17
(November 1971).

50. O'Flaherty, Liam. The Terrorist. London:
E. Archer, 1926.

51. Pepper, Curtis B. "The Possessed." New York
Times Magazine, February 18, 1979, 29-32ff.

A journalistic account of the rise of the
Brigate Rosse, including biographical data on
its founder Renato Curcio.

52. _____. Kidnapped! 17 Days of Terror. New
York: Harmony, 1978.

A narrative account of the 1978 kidnapping
of Paolo Lazzaroni, 40 year old son of a
wealthy Milanese manufacturer. The kidnapping,
apparently carried out by the Mafia, was yet
another example of the rash of kidnappings-
for-profit which have been so much a feature of
contemporary Italy.

53. Price, D.L. Institute for the Study of Conflict. Ulster: Consensus and Coercion.
London: Idem, 1973.

Most noteworthy for its examination of the
effects of government security activities on
the tactics of the terrorist in Northern Ireland.

54. Provisional IRA. _Freedom Struggle_. Irish Republican Publicity Bureau, June 30, 1973.

    Includes a list of IRA dead.

55. Ronchey, Alberto. "Terror in Italy: Between Red and Black." _Dissent_, (Spring 1978) 150-156.

56. _____. "Guns and Gray Matter: Terrorism in Italy." _Foreign Affairs_, 37 (Spring 1978), 921-940.

57. Stafford, David. "Anarchists in Britain Today." _Government and Opposition_, 6 (1971): 345-353.

58. Street, M. "Prevention of Terrorism (Temporary Provisions) Act of 1974." _Criminal Law Review_ (London, April 1975, 192-199.

    A critical assessment of British legislation to control terrorist activities related to Northern Ireland.

59. Sundberg, Jacob. "The Antiterrorist Legislation in Sweden." pp. 111-121, in Livingston, ed.

60. Terchek, Ronald. "Conflict and Cleavage in Northern Ireland." _Annals_, no. 433 (September 1977): 47-59.

    Useful as background material, rather than as a vehicle for studying terrorism in Northern Ireland. Terchek traces the conflict to the conflicts between the Protestant and Catholic communities, as well as the strains produced by any attempt to include the Catholic minority in the government.

61. United Kingdom. _Report of the Committee of Privy Counsellors Appointed to Consider Authorized Procedures for the Interrogation of Persons Suspected of Terrorism_. London, 1972.

62. Van Voris, W.H. _Violence in Ulster: An Oral_

<u>Documentary</u>. Amherst: University of Massachusetts Press, 1975.

63. Young, Rochfort, and Adams, John. <u>Case for Detention</u>. London: Bow Publications, <u>1974</u>.

Argues for continuance of detention without trial in Northern Ireland as long as the judicial system continues to be ineffective.

ADDENDUM

Dillon, Martin, and Lehane, D. <u>Political Mur-der in Northern Ireland</u>. Harmondsworth: Penguin, 1973.

(unseen)

Lebow, Richard N. "The Origins of Sectarian Assassination: The Case of Belfast." <u>Journal of International Affairs</u>, 32 (Spring/Summer 1978): 43-61.

Silj, Alessandro. <u>Never Again Without a Rifle: The Origins of Italian Terrorism</u>. NY: Karz, 1979.

Wagenlehner, Gunther. "Motivation for Political Terrorism in Germany." In Entry A117, 195-203.

Section P
Eastern Europe and the Soviet Union

1. Barton, M. "International Terrorism." Review
   of International Affairs, 23 (April 20,
   1972): 25.

2. Bilinsky, Yaroslav. "The Background of Contemporary Politics in the Baltic Republic and
   the Ukraine: Comparisons and Contrasts."
   In Problems of Mininations: Baltic Perspectives edited by Arvids Ziedonia, Jr.;
   Rein Taagepara; and Mardi Valgemae. San
   Jose: California State University, Association for the Advancement of Baltic
   Studies, Inc., 1973.

   (Unseen)

3. Institute for the Study of Conflict. "Croat
   Separatism: Nationalism, Dissidence and
   Terrorism." Conflict Studies, 103 (Jan-
   uary 1979).

   An up-to-date overview Croatian resistance
   to the concept and the reality of Yugoslavia.
   Begins with the founding of the Ustase, surveys
   the wartime Croat state, post-war subversion,
   links to Moscow, and the activities of the
   1970's. Projects enhanced separtist militancy
   (hence: terrorism) in the post-Tito era.

4. Paris, Edmund. Genocide in Satellite Croatia,
   1941-1945. A Record of Racial and Religious
   Persecutions and Massacres. Trans. by Lois
   Perkins. Chicago, IL: The American Institute for Balkan Affairs, 1961.

   The title accurately reflects the slant of

this book.

5. Romaniecki, Leon. "The Soviet Union and Inter-
        national Terrorism." Soviet Studies (Uni-
        versity of Glascow), 24 (July 1974):
        417-440.

    (Unseen)

6. Tomasic, Dinko. "The Ustasha Movement."
        Slavonic Encyclopedia. New York: Kennikat
        Press, 1949, 1337-1341.

7. Zivic, J. "The Nonaligned and the Problem of
        International Terrorism." Review of In-
        ternational Affairs. (Belgrade), 24
        (January 20, 1973): 6-8.

    (Unseen)

Section Q
Terrorist Internationale?

(See appropriate topical sections, e.g., for Soviet
        support of fedayeen, see M.E.)

1. Barron, John. KGB: the Soviet Work of Soviet
        Secret Agents. New York: Bantam, 1974.

    (Passim)

2. Clutterbuck, Richard. "Terrorist Internation-
        al." Army Quarterly, 104 (January 1974):
        154-159.

    (Unseen)

3. Friedlander, Robert A. "Reflections on Ter-
        rorist Havens." Naval War College Review,
        32 (March-April 1979): 59-67.

        "Terrorism does not depend on the existance
    of havens for terrorists but would not have
    been as prevalent nor extensive a phenomenon
    as it has been, absent those havens. This and
    the terrorist threat to world public order are
    generally agreed. Little else, not prosriptive
    measures nor even definitions, is agreed" [edi-
    tor's headnote].

4. Institute for the Study of Conflict. "The
        Surrogate Forces of the Soviet Union."
        Conflict Studies Security Report, 92 (Feb-
        ruary 1978).

        See esp. pp 5-7, "Surrogate terrorists and
    guerrillas," and the "Role of Libya."

5. Weber, Tom. "The Strange Capital of World
        Terrorism." "The Strategy for World Wide
        Guerrilla War." "Man Behind the War
        Against South Africa." "Guerrilla's War

Warning for Marcos." "Why Africans Trust
Envoy Young." <u>San Francisco Chronicle</u>,
9, 10, 11, 12, <u>13 October 1978.</u>

A "special report" from Tripoli, Libya,
"meeting place of the world's revolutionary
gun slingers...and terrorists who call themselves 'freedom fighters'." A fascinating
account.

6. Wolf, John B. "Global Terrorist Coalition:
Its Incipient Stage." <u>Police Journal</u>,
(England) 50 (October-December 1977):
328-339.

Section R
Combating Terrorism:
Macro-Perspectives

1. Beaumont, Roger A. "Military Elite Forces:
   Surrogate War, Terrorism, and the New Bat-
   tlefield." Parameters, Journal of the
   U.S. Army War College, 9 (March 1979):
   17-29.

   A useful overview of the historical and contemporary role of elite forces, which have
   recently been used with some success to counter
   terrorism. The growth of such forces from
   170,000 in 1974 to almost a million in 1977,
   indicates the pertinence of the topic.

2. Bishop, Joseph W., Jr. "Can Democracy Defend
   Itself Against Terrorism." Commentary,
   May 1978, pp. 55-62.

   A useful, if marginally polemical, treatment of the legal and extra-legal adaptations
   which have been made in Northern Ireland by
   the Stormont and the British government.
   Bishop compares the remedies that have been applied in North Ireland to those that might be
   adopted by the U.S. in a period of intense terrorist activity. He concludes that the use of
   juryless trials, relaxation of rules of evidence and the burden of proof, and the crime
   of association would raise grave constitutional
   issues. Arguing from stare decisis he asserts
   that an important legitimate power would be
   the use of armed force. He finds that intern-
   ment is probably constitutional, as might be
   the juryless trial (in the model from the
   "Diplock Courts" and in North Ireland). Bishop's argument for preemptive reaction to be
   applied selectively, in order to prevent rescue

operations will no doubt be troubling to civil
libertarians and those who oppose capital punishment on principle. Letter to the Editor
and Bishop's reply, appearing in Commentary,
August 1978, should be read in conjunction
with the article.

3. Bouza, A. V. Police Intelligence: the Opera-
    tions of an Investigative Unit (New York
    City). New York: AMS Press, Inc., 1976.

    (Unseen)

4. Bowden, Tom. Men in the Middle--The U.K.
    Police. London: Institute for the Study
    of Conflict, 1976.

    A treatment of the problems terrorism pre-
    sents for police in Britain, and the solutions
    adopted.

5. Browne, Jeffrey T. International Terrorism:
    the American Response. Washington, D. C.:
    the American University, School of Inter-
    national Service, December 1973.

6. Civiletti, Benjamin R. "Terrorism: the Gov-
    ernment's Response Policy." FBI Law En-
    forcement Journal, January 1979, pp. 19-22.

    Excerpted from testimony to the Congress,
    on August 16, 1978. Civiletti is the Deputy
    Attorney General, and as such has been dele-
    gated the responsibility to oversee government
    responses to acts of terrorism. He presents
    a basically optimistic perspective on the cap-
    ability of the U.S. government to counter-
    terror, while he admits that "upgrading" may
    be necessary in some areas (e.g., military
    training and special equipment). Some details
    of the organization of the government's coun-
    ter-terrorism structure are provided.

7. Clutterbuck, Richard. "Police and Urban Ter-
    rorism." Police Journal (England) 48
    (July-September 1975): 204-214.

8. Cooper, H. H. A. Hostage Rescue Operations:
    Denouement at Algeria and Mogadishu Com-
    pared." Chitty's Law Journal, 26 (March
    1978): 91-104.

9. Cooper, H.H.A. "Terrorism and the Intelligence
    Function." Chitty's Law Journal 73 (March
    1976): 24ff.

    Cooper presents a brief and general dis-
    cussion of the function of intelligence in
    countering terrorism. He argues that a careful
    distinction should be drawn between intelli-
    gence, counter-intelligence, and preventive
    intelligence functions in light of the abuses
    which have been revealed and the resultant
    concern for eliminating excesses. By clearly
    distinguishing the one function from the other,
    the intelligence agencies (with adequate guide-
    lines) will avoid the "contamination" which
    programs such as Cointelpro generated, and will
    be able to continue exercising the intelligence
    function," which Cooper argues is of the utmost
    importance in combating terrorism.

10. Corves, Erich. "International Cooperation in
    the Field of International Political Ter-
    rorism." Terrorism. 1 (1978): 199-210.

    An overview.

11. Crelinsten, Ronald D.; Laberge-Altmejd, D. and
    Svabo, D. Terrorism and Criminal Justice:
    An International Perspective. Lexington,
    Mass: Heath Lexington Books, 1978.

    A LEAA-sponsored study, provides data from
    Belgium, Finland, France, U.S., Sweden, Germany
    and Northern Ireland. The diversity of anti-
    terror national policies is demonstrated.

12. Evans, Ernest. "American Policy Response to
    International Terrorism: Problems of De-
    terrence." In Entry A4, 106-117.

13. _____. "American Policy Response to Inter-
    national Terrorism: Problems of Deter-
    rence. In Entry A117, 376-385.

14. Fogel, Lawrence J. Predictive Antiterrorism.
    Decision Sciences, Inc., April 1977.

    (Unseen)

15. Gregory, Frank. Protest and Violence: the
    Police Response--A Comparative Analysis

of Democratic Methods. London: Institute for the Study of Conflict, 1976.

A sketchy account, including case material from France, West Germany, Italy, Japan, U.K. and the U.S.

16. Hoffacker, Lewis. "The Government Response to Terrorism: A Global Approach." U.S. Department of State Bulletin, 70 (March 18, 1974): 274-278. (Reprinted in Entry A12)

17. Kitson, Frank. Low Intensity Operations: Subversion, Insurgency & Peacekeeping. Harrisburg, PA: Stackpole Books, 1971.

18. Lopez, Vincent C. What the U.S. Army Should Do About Urban Guerrilla Warfare. Springfield, VA: National Technical Information Center, 1975.

19. McCormick, R.W. "Industrial Security in Europe: A Multinational Concept." Security Management, 18 (July 1974): 8-10f.

20. McDowell, Charles P. and Harlan, John P. "Police Response to Political Crimes and Acts of Terrorism: Some Dimensions for Consideration." Paper delivered to the American Society of Criminology annual meeting, Toronto, Canada, October 30, November 2, 1975.

21. Roberts, Kenneth E. Terrorism and the Military Response. Carlisle Barracks, PA: Army War College Strategic Studies Institute, October, 1975.

22. Sloan, Stephen. "Simulating Terrorism: From Operational Technique to Questions of Policy." International Studies Notes, 5 (Winter 1978): 3-8.

23. Smith, R.D., and Kobetz, R. Guidelines for Civil Disorders and Mobilization Planning. Gaithenburg, Md.: International Association of Chiefs of Police, 1968.

24. Steinhilper, G. Violence and Police. Strasbourg, France: Council of Europe, European Committee on Crime, 1977.

25. Tanham, George K.; Jenkins, Brian; Wainstein,
     Eleanor S.; and Sullivan, Gerald. "United
     States Preparation for Future Low-Level
     Conflict." Conflict: An International
     Journal for Conflict and Policy Studies,
     1 (1978): 1-19.

          Report of a meeting held in Washington,
     at the Rand Corporation, in October 1976. The
     subject was the ability of the U.S. to respond
     to the low-level conflicts which are consider-
     ed likely to define parameters for the re-
     mainder of the century. In nearly every realm,
     the participants (Government officials and
     think-tank professionals) found the U.S. capa-
     bility to be inadequate. Recommendations in-
     clude a centralized organization to cope with
     low-level conflict; enhanced contingency plan-
     ning, and gaming by top level officials; in-
     creased emphasis within the services; further
     coordination with allies; and a partial re-
     direction of intelligence efforts.

26. U. S. Department of Justice. Law Enforcement
     Assistance Administration. Private Secur-
     ity Advisory Council. Prevention of Ter-
     roristic Crimes: Security Guidelines for
     Business, Industry, and other Organiza-
     tions. Washington, D.C., May 1976.

27. Wahl, Jonathan. "Responses to Terrorism:
     Self-Defense or Reprisal?" International
     Problems, 5, Nos. 1-2 (1973): 28-33.

     (Unseen)

28. Wolf, John B. "Controlling Political Terror-
     ism in a Free Society." Orbis, 19 (Winter
     1976): 1289-1308.

Section S
Combating Terrorism:
Micro-Perspectives

1. Adkins, E.H., Jr. "Protection of American In-
    dustrial Dignitaries and Facilities Over-
    seas." Security Management, 18 (July
    1974): 14-ff.

2. Allbach, D.M. "Countering Special-Threat Sit-
    uations." Military Police Law Enforcement
    Journal, 2 (Summer 1975): 34-40.

3. DeBecker, Gavin. "Protecting VIP's (Very Im-
    portant Persons), Part 1." Counterforce, 1
    (March 1977): 11-14.

4. Epstein, D.G. "Combatting Campus Terrorism."
    Police Chief, January 1971, 46, 47 and 49.

    Guidance for campus police.

5. Fulton, Arthur B. Countermeasures to Combat
    Terrorism at Major Events. Washington:
    U.S. Dept. of State, 1976.

    Includes treatment of the Black September
    attack at the Munich Olympics, as well as the
    security preparations for the 1976 Olympics.

6. Fuqua, Paul and Wilson, Jerry. Terrorism:
    The Executive's Guide to Survival.
    Houston: Gulf Publishing Co., 1978.

7. Mahoney, M.T. "After a Terrorist Attack:
    Business as Usual." Security Management,
    19 (March 1975): 16-ff.

8. Rayne, F. "Executive Protection and Terrorism."
    Top Security (England) 1 (October 1975):

220-225.

9. Robinson, W.S. "University Confrontation: A Philosophy of University Policy Strategy, Confrontation, Tactics and Equipment." Police Chief, January 1971, 26-33.

10. Scotti, Tony. "Countermeasure: Protective Driving." Counterforce, 1 (March 1977): 17-18.

11. Security Gazette. "Aids to the Detection of Explosives--A Brief Review of Equipment for Searching Out Letter Bombs and Other Explosive Devices." Idem. 17 (February 1975): 48-49f.

12. Shaw, P.D. "Extortion Threats: Analytic Techniques and Resources." Assets Protection, 1 (Summer 1975): 5-16.

A description of the phenomena of extortion complemented by a discussion of preventive and identification procedures.

13. Shriver, R.B., Jr.; Evans, J.C.; and Leibstone, M. Countering Terrorism on Military Installations: Final Report (to the Department of the Army). McLean, VA: Science Applications, Inc., 1977.

14. Silverstein, Martin E. "Emergency Medical Preparedness." Terrorism, 1 (1977): 51-69.

15. _____. Medical Reserve as an Anti-terrorist Measure. Prepared for the Law Enforcement Assistance Administration and delivered at the Seminar on Research Strategies for the Study of International Political Terrorism, Evian, France, June 1977.

16. Singer, L.W. "New Way to Face Terrorists: A Crisis Management System." Security Management, 21 (September 1977): 6-9ff.

17. U.S. Department of the Army. Personal Security Precaution Against Acts of Terrorism. Washington, D.C.: 1977.

Practical information and advice.

18. Wolf, John B. "Police Intelligence: Focus for Counter-Terrorist Operations." <u>Police Journal</u> (England), 49 (January-March 1976): 19-27.

Section T
Surveys of the Literature

1. Avishai, Bernard. "In Cold Blood". The New
    York Review of Books, March 8, 1979, 41-44.

    A very critical review of Bell (Entry A15),
    Schreiber (A170) and Hirst (Addendum) by an
    Israeli professor of political philosophy.
    Avishai attacks Bell and Schreiber in particu-
    lar for their alleged moral relativism, even
    reticence, regarding normative arguments
    raised by terrorism.

2. Bell, J. Bowyer. "Trends on Terror: The Ana-
    lysis of Political Violence." World Poli-
    tics, XXIX (April 1977): 476-488.

    A masterful bibliographic essay.

3. Friedlander, Robert A. Review of Interna-
    tional Terrorism and Political Crimes
    edited by M. Cherif Bassiouni. Revue
    Internationale de Droit Penal, 46 (1975):
    523-527. (In English)

    Not just a book review, but a competent
    essay on the subject.

4. _____. "History as Demonology". [Review
    of: Terrorism: From Robespierre to Ara-
    fat by Albert Parry.] Saint Louis Univer-
    sity Law Journal, 22 (1978): 233-242.

    On the problems of subjectivism in the
    description of terrorism.

5. Gross, Bernard. "Terrorism and Literature".
    In Entry A117, 447-453.

6. Miller, Abraham H. "On Terrorism". Public
    Administration Review, July/August 1977,
    429-435.

    Comprehensive review essay treating works
    by Yonah Alexander, J. Bowyer Bell, and Chris-
    topher Dobson. Miller criticizes the litera-
    ture in general, for its failure to address
    the public policy aspects of the terrorism
    problem.

7. Norton, Augustus R. "Terrorism: Understanding
    the Phenomena". Forthcoming in Armed
    Forces and Society.

8. Spjut, R. J. "Review of Counter-Insurgency
    Theorists." Political Quarterly (England),
    49 (January-March 1978): 54-64.

    (unseen)

Section U
Terrorism in Fiction

This section concentrates on important or interesting fictional treatments of terrorism, drawn primarily from the 1976 to 1978 period, three years that witnessed an enormous proliferation of this type of book.

1. Albert, Marvin. The Gargoyle Conspiracy. Garden City, N.Y.: Doubleday, 1975.

   An interesting assassination plot directed against the American Secretary of State. The terrorists are Arabs.

2. Ambler, Eric. The Levanter. New York: Atheneum, 1972.

   This novel features the planning of terrorist attacks on Tel Aviv by Palestinians.

3. Ardies, Tom. Kosygin is Coming. Garden City, N.Y.: Doubleday, 1974.

4. _____. This Suitcase is Going to Explode. Garden City, N.Y.: Doubleday, 1973.

   A nuclear blackmail novel in which a group plants nuclear devices in suitcases in selected sites in the United States.

5. Arrighi, Mel. Navona 1000. Indianapolis: Bobbs-Merrill, 1976.

6. Arvay, Harry. Operation Kuwait. New York: Bantam, 1975.

An anti-terrorist novel featuring Israeli intelligence attempts to foil skyjacking by des-
troying the training facilities of the terrorists.

7. _____. *The Piraeus Plot*. New York: Bantam,
     1975.

An interesting novel in which Israel <u>assists</u>
Yasser Arafat in maintaining power against his
more radical rivals.

8. Atles, Philip. *The Underground Cities Contract*.
     New York: Pinnacle Books, 1974.

Interesting only because it is one of the
very few fictional treatments of Turkish terrorists.

9. Atwater, James D. *Time Bomb*. New York:
     Viking, 1977.

Exciting novel which contains detailed accounts of dismantling IRA bombs. The author
spent time with British units engaged in the
task.

10. Awin, Margery. *Silence Over Sinai*. New York:
     Pyramid, 1976.

Arab terrorists plot to seize the Israeli
and Egyptian leaders at a secret summit meeting.
The main protaganist is an "Arabist" from the
State Department.

11. Ballard, J. G. *High Rise*. New York: Holt,
     1977.

12. Black, Lionel. *Arafat Is Next!* New York:
     Stein & Day, 1975.

Anti-terrorist activity, including an attempt
on the life of Yasser Arafat, conducted by <u>pri-
vate</u> individuals.

13. Burmeister, Jon. *Running Scared*. New York:
     St. Martin's Press, 1973.

14. Caidin, Martin. *Almost Midnight*. New York:
     Morrow, 1971.

An exciting novel of nuclear blackmail (including the theft of nuclear weapons) by the creator of the "Six Million Dollar Man."

15. _____. Operation Nuke. New York: McKay, 1973.

   Similar to the above book, and not as realistic.

16. Caillou, Alan. Death Charge. New York: Pinnacle Books, 1973.

   Mercenaries are employed to counter Mexican terrorists. The kidnapping scenes are generally well done.

17. Callison, Brian. A Plague of Sailors. New York: Putnam, 1971.

18. Calmer, Ned. The Peking Dimension. Garden City, N.Y.: Doubleday, 1976.

   Excellent novel involving the kidnapping of the daughter of an American diplomat and of a Chinese diplomat, with the Middle East as the ultimate goal.

19. Carroll, James. Madonna Red. Boston: Little, Brown, 1976.

20. Chandler, David T. The Capablanca Opening. New York: St. Martin's, 1977.

   A good novel featuring the Tupamaro guerrillas and kidnapping.

21. Charles, Robert. Flight of the Raven. New York: Pinnacle Books, 1975.

22. _____. The Hour of the Wolf. New York: Pinnacle Books, 1975.

   A prototypical paperback thriller which features "Terror, Inc." and efforts to counter its activities.

23. Condon, Richard. The Whisper of the Axe. New York: Dial, 1976.

   Excellent Black revolution novel which in-

cludes the funding of terrorism through the
drug trade with the cooperation of Haitian
leaders. The book contains excellent insights
into urban warfare.

24. Cox, Richard. Sam Seven. New York: Reader's
     Digest Press, 1977.

An excellent novel involving the shooting
down of an airliner by a heat seeking missile.
Obviously based on the possibility that attempts have already taken place.

25. Crosby, John. An Affair of Strangers. New
     York: Stein & Day, 1975.

26. Dan, Uri, and Peter Mann. Ultimatum: Pu 94.
     New York: Leisure Books, 1977.

Terrorists attempt to construct a nuclear
weapon. Interesting because of the references
to actual articles on nuclear terrorism.

27. Delaney, Laurence. The Triton Ultimatum. New
     York: Crowell, 1977.

Concerns the takeover of a U.S. nuclear bal-
listic missile submarine. The author was a
former submarine officer, and this book reportedly led to the planning of the real thing.

28. De Mille, Nelson. By the Rivers of Babylon.
     New York: Harcourt Brace, 1978.

An attempt by Palestinians to subvert an Arab-
Israeli peace conference leads to the downing
of the aircraft carrying the Israeli delegation.
The action involves attempts to capture the delegation on the ground.

29. DiMona, Joseph. The Benedict Arnold Connection.
     New York: Morrow, 1977.

Nuclear weapons theft, involving a member of
the U.S. President's Cabinet, is well portrayed
in an exciting novel.

30. Driscoll, Peter. In Connection with Kilshaw.
     Philadelphia: Lippincott, 1974.

31. Duncan, Robert L. Fire Storm. New York:

Morrow, 1978.

American oil magnates attempt to assassinate a Senator by using Japanese terrorists armed with a hugh tanker.

32. Fairbairn, Douglas. _Street 8_. New York: Delacorte, 1977.

An excellent novel involving Cuban anti-Castro terrorists.

33. Fleming, H.K. _The Day They Kidnapped Queen Victoria_. New York: St. Martin's, 1978.

Irish nationalists kidnap the Queen and attempt to take her to Ireland by ship. An excellent and credible book.

34. Fleming, Ian. _On Her Majesty's Secret Service_. New York: New American Library, 1963.

The famous James Bond in a novel of nuclear blackmail. This is one of the better novels in the series.

35. Flynn, J.M. _Warlock_. New York: Pocket Books, 1976.

36. Forbes, Colin. _Year of the Golden Ape_. New York: Dutton, 1974.

Complicated but interesting novel involving a nuclear weapon on an oil tanker, with the goal of fomenting an oil boycott against the West. The concept of using terror (and the threat of terror) to manipulate public opinion is well presented.

37. Frankel, Sandor, and Webster Mews. _The Aleph Solution_. New York: Stein & Day, 1978.

An exciting account of the seizure of the General Assembly of the United Nations by Palestinian terrorists and attempts to defeat their plan. The authors carefully examined security measures at the U.N.

38. Gill, Bartholomew. _McGarr and the Politician's Wife_. New York: Scribners, 1977.

A wonderful novel of the "Irish Question,"
with insights on the psychology of terrorism.

39. Gilman, Dorothy. <u>Mrs. Pollifax on Safari</u>.
    Garden City, N.Y.: Doubleday, 1977.

    Terrorism in Zambia. An interesting book
    with a fine touch of humor.

40. Godey, John. <u>The Talisman</u>. New York: Putnam,
    1976.

    Vietnam veterans threaten to destroy the re-
    mains of the Unknown Soldier unless the Presi-
    dent pardons a leading anti-war activist.

41. Graves, Richard L. <u>C.L.A.W.</u> New York: Stein
    & Day, 1976.

    Features attacks on candidates during an
    American election campaign by U.S. trained
    Vietnamese working for an anarchist organization.
    There is also an interesting plot to attack
    during the Inauguration of the President.

42. _____. <u>Cobalt 60</u>. New York: Stein & Day,
    1975.

    One of the better counter-terrorist novels.

43. Haddad, C.A. <u>Bloody September</u>. New York:
    Harper & Row, 1976.

44. Hall, Adam. <u>The Kobra Manifesto</u>. Garden City,
    N.Y.: Doubleday, 1976.

    An exciting novel that includes aerial pir-
    acy, the kidnapping of the daughter of the
    American Secretary of Defense, and PLO opera-
    tives.

45. Harris, Tom. <u>Black Sunday</u>. New York: Putnam,
    1975.

    An outstanding novel of its type, this famous
    book is exciting but not quite convincing. The
    attack on the Super Bowl Game (by blimp) is well
    thought out, but the real value of the novel
    lies in its portrayal of the psychology of the
    terrorist and those who fight him. It was the

subject of an excellent film.

46. Harrison, Harry. Queen Victoria's Revenge.
    Garden City, N.Y.: Doubleday, 1975.

    One of the earliest novels to emphasize coop-
    eration between terrorist groups and cooperation
    between those who combat them.

47. Hartley, Norman. The Viking Process. New York:
    Simon and Schuster, 1976.

    An anti-multinational corporation novel which
    features considerable violence and wild terro-
    rist acts, including an attack on a London
    hotel.

48. Hebden, Mark. March of Violence. New York:
    Harcourt, 1970.

49. Henissart, Paul. Narrow Exit. New York: Simon
    & Schuster, 1974.

50. Herron, Shaun. Through the Dark and Hairy Wood.
    New York: Random House, 1972.

51. Hesky, Olga. A Different Night. New York:
    Random House, 1971.

52. Higgins, Jack. The Savage Day. New York:
    Holt, 1972.

    An excellent novel which features the supply
    of arms to the Irish Republican Army.

53. _____. Wrath of the Lion. Greenwich, Conn.:
    Fawcett, 1977.

    Originally written in 1964, this is a good
    novel of the French right-wing and the reaction
    in that country to the struggles in Algeria and
    Indochina.

54. Himmel, Richard. The Twenty-Third Web. New
    York: Random House, 1977.

    The plot involves the planting of terrorists
    in dozens of American cities in an attempt to
    stop financial support for Israel. Not alto-
    gether implausible.

55. Hoffenberg, Jack. <u>17 Ben Gurion</u>. New York:
    Putnam, 1977.

    A novel of Middle East terrorism, with ob-
    vious parallels to real figures and events. An
    extremely well-plotted book.

56. Household, Geoffrey. <u>High Place</u>. Boston:
    Little, Brown, 1955.

57. _____. <u>Hostage: London</u>. Boston: Atlantic
    Monthly-Little, Brown, 1977.

    The countering of a plot to construct a nu-
    clear weapon in London. Household has done
    better, but this is still an excellent novel.

58. Jepson, Selwyn. <u>A Noise in the Night</u>. Phila-
    delphia: Lippincott, 1957.

59. Kalb, Marvin, and Ted Koppel. <u>In the National
    Interest</u>. New York: Simon & Schuster, 1977.

    Involves the kidnapping of the wife of the
    American Secretary of State while he is engaged
    in "shuttle diplomacy" in the Middle East. The
    story revolves around determining who did it.

60. Kane, Henry. <u>The Tripoli Documents</u>. New York:
    Simon and Schuster, 1976.

    A plot to assassinate the American Secretary
    of State by a Palestinian "hit man," who is
    also responsible for the death of Robert
    Kennedy.

61. Katz, Robert. <u>Ziggurat</u>. Boston: Houghton
    Mifflin, 1977.

    A home-made nuclear weapon novel, especially
    strong on the use of publicity in terrorism,
    and on security arrangements in nuclear plants.

62. Lambert, Derek. <u>The Yermakov Transfer</u>. New
    York: Saturday Review Press, 1974.

    One of the relatively few novels featuring
    the use of terror and blackmail against the
    Soviet Union, this book has Jewish activists
    out to kidnap the Soviet Premier with the goal
    of forcing the authorities to allow the emigra-

191

tion of key Jews to Israel.

63. Lippincott, David. *The Voice of Armageddon*. New York: Putnam, 1974.

64. Lyall, Gavin. *Judas Country*. New York: Viking, 1975.

65. McAlister, Ian. *Strike Force 7*. Greenwich, Conn.: Fawcett, 1974.

   Features the use of mercenaries as anti-terrorist operatives.

66. McClure, James. *Rogue Eagle*. New York: Harper & Row, 1976.

   Terrorism in South Africa, with the terrorists belonging to an extremist white organization.

67. McDonald, Hugh C. *Five Signs From Ruby*. New York: Pyramid, 1976.

   The PLO funds the construction of five nuclear weapons. The designer then blackmails the Israelis, as they search for the devices. A very exciting read.

68. MacLean, Alistair. *Goodbye California*. Garden City, N.Y.: Doubleday, 1978.

   A nuclear power plant takeover novel, with the object the creation of a nuclear earthquake that will destroy California.

69. Marshall, William. *Gelignite*. New York: Holt, 1977.

   Terrorists threaten to destroy the Chinese cemetery in Hong Kong, thus depriving the dead of eternity according to religious beliefs. A very different choice of target makes this an interesting book.

70. Mason, Colin. *Hostage*. New York: Walker, 1973.

   American nuclear weapons stolen by Israeli militants destroy Cairo. The novel centers on the Soviet response, which involves counter-city strategies.

71. Mills, James. <u>The Seventh Power</u>. New York: Dutton, 1976.

    This novel contains a detailed discussion of how to build a nuclear weapon in your basement.

72. Naipaul, V.S. <u>Guerrillas</u>. New York: Knopf, 1975.

73. O'Neill, Edward A. <u>The Rotterdam Delivery</u>. New York: Coward, 1975.

    An oil tanker hijacking caper. The goals of the hijackers are financial, not political.

74. Osmond, Andrew. <u>Saladin!</u> Garden City, N.Y.: Doubleday, 1976.

    The action takes place around the 1972 Munich massacre, and involves a Palestinian attempt to destroy the headquarters of Israeli intelligence.

75. Pace, Eric. <u>Any War Will Do</u>. New York: Random House, 1972.

76. Parker, Robert B. <u>The Judas Goat</u>. Boston: Houghton Mifflin, 1978.

    An excellent urban terror novel. The terrorists are right-wing Americans, and the book has an exciting climax at the 1976 Olympic Games.

77. Pitts, Denis. <u>This City Is Ours</u>. New York: Mason Charter, 1975.

    Yet another oil tanker caper. New York will be destroyed unless payment is made.

78. Price, Anthony. <u>The Alamut Bomb</u>. Garden City, N.Y.: Doubleday, 1972.

    One of the best and most neglected "Palestinian Terrorist Novels."

79. Rayner, William. <u>Day of Chaminuka</u>. New York: Atheneum, 1977.

80. Ritner, Peter. _The Passion of Richard Thynne_.
    New York: Morrow, 1976.

    Interesting only because of the terrorist, a
    Native American, and the choice of targets--for
    example, the Widener Library.

81. Ross, Frank. _Dead Runner_. New York: Atheneum,
    1977.

    Arab terrorists and nuclear blackmail. The
    goal is the release of an Arab terrorist in
    British hands.

82. Rowe, James N. _The Judas Squad_. Boston:
    Little, Brown, 1977.

    An excellent examination of nuclear theft
    and hostage bargaining. One of the best re-
    searched novels of its type.

83. Sanders, Leonard. _The Hamlet Warning_. New
    York: Scribners, 1976.

    International terrorists attempt to construct
    a nuclear device in the Dominican Republic.
    Sanders is always worth reading.

84. Sapir, Richard and Warren Murphy. _The Terror
    Squad_. New York: Pinnacle Books, 1973.

    One of a series of novels which runs into
    the dozens and which features "The Destroyer,"
    this is an interesting account of international
    terrorist collaboration.

85. Seaman, Donald. _The Terror Syndicate_. New
    York: Coward, McCann, 1976.

86. Sela, Owen. _An Exchange of Eagles_. New York:
    Pantheon, 1977.

    An excellent novel that uses real-life his-
    torical figures in a story that never sags. An
    attempt to prevent World War II by assassina-
    tion.

87. Seymour, Gerald. _The Glory Boys_. New York:
    Random House, 1976.

    Outstanding for its detailed presentation of

the evolution of a terrorist act, this time to
be carried out by a Palestinian-IRA team.

88. _____. Kingfisher. New York: Summit
       Books, 1978.

   An excellent and well written skyjacking
novel. The terrorists are Jews attempting to
flee the Soviet Union.

89. Theroux, Paul. The Family Arsenal. Boston:
       Houghton Mifflin, 1976.

   This best-selling novel dramatically por-
trays a London-based cell of the modern IRA.
Notable for its caricature of the mundane life
of terrorists.

90. Washburn, Mark. The Armageddon Game. New
       York: Putnam, 1977.

   Another let's build a nuclear weapon story,
strong on psychology, with some interesting
things to say about the 1960's.

91. Watkins, Leslie. The Killing of Idi Amin. New
       York: Avon, 1977.

   "Sanity International" attempts to assassinate Amin for the sake of humanity.

92. Williams, Alan. Shah-Mak. New York: Coward,
       McCann, 1976.

   The plot involves a fake assassination intended to discredit political enemies in a
mythical Mideast Kingdom. The attempt turns
into the real thing. Most interesting for its
account of the manipulation of terrorism for
other goals.

93. Williamson, Tony. The Doomsday Contract. New
       York: Simon & Schuster, 1978.

   A wild story in which attempts are made to
hijack nuclear weapons, kidnap nuclear scientists for purposes of building nuclear weapons,
and steal plutonium.

94. Wingate, John. Avalanche. New York: St.
       Martin's, 1977.

195

95. Wolfe, Michael. The Panama Paradox. New York: Harper & Row, 1977.

    Highly recommended novel involving Panamanian terrorist attacks against the Panama Canal. The book contains several scenarios for attacking and defending the Canal.

96. Wylie, Philip. The Smuggled Atom Bomb. Garden City, N.Y.: Doubleday, 1965.

    One of the last books by the noted author of A Generation of Vipers, it is still one of the better nuclear blackmail stories.

97. Wyllie, John. Death Is A Drum . . . Beating Forever. Garden City, N.Y.: Doubleday, 1977.

98. Yates, Brock. Dead In the Water. New York: Farrar, 1975.

    An excellent novel about an attempt to kidnap the Prime Minister of Canada.

99. Yerby, Frank. A Rose for Ana Maria. New York: Dial, 1976.

ADDENDUM

Freeling, Nicolas. Gadget. Harmondsworth: Penguin Books, 1977.

    The kidnapping of a nuclear physicist by terrorists (for the obvious reason). This novel was apparently ghost-written in large part by an American nuclear physicist.

Fuentes, Carlos. The Hydra Head, trans. by Margaret Sayers Penden. New York: Farrar, Straus & Giroux, 1978.

Section V
Terror Campaigns

1. Conquest, Robert. <u>The Great Terror</u>. New
    York: Macmillan, 1973.

2. Dallin, Alexander and Breslauce, George W.
    <u>Political Terror in Communist Systems.</u>
    Stanford, Calif.: Stanford University
    Press, 1970.

    Includes a 16 page bibliography.

3. Gross, Feliks. <u>Violence in Politics: Terror
    and Political Assassination in Eastern
    Europe and Russia</u>. The Hague: Mouton,
    1972.
4. Merleau-Ponty, Maurice. <u>Humanism and Terror:
    An Essay on the Communist Problem,</u> trans.
    by J. O'Neill. Boston: Beacon Press,
    1969.

5. Moore, Barrington M., Jr. <u>Terror and Progress
    in the U.S.S.R.</u> Cambridge, Mass.: Har-
    vard University Press, 1954.

6. Rosenbaum, H. Jon, and Sederberg, Peter C.
    "Vigilantism: An Analysis of Establish-
    ment Violence." <u>Comparative Politics</u>, 6
    (1974): 541-570.

7. Solzhenitsyn, Alexander. <u>The Gulag Archipela-
    go</u>, I, II, III. New York: Harper and
    Row, 1974-1978.

8. Walter, Eugene V. <u>Terror and Resistance: A
    Study of Political Violence, with Case
    Studies of Some Primitive African Communi-</u>

ties. New York: Oxford University, 1969.

9. _____. "Violence and the Process of Terror."
American Sociological Review, 29 (April
1964): 248-257.

Section W
Bibliographies

1. Blackey, Robert. <u>Modern Revolutions and Revo-</u>
    <u>lutionists: A Bibliography</u>. Santa Bar-
    bara, Calif., Clio Books, 1976.

2. Boston, Guy D; O'Brien, Kevin; and Palumbo,
    Joanne. <u>Terrorism: A Selected Biblio-</u>
    <u>graphy</u>. Washington, Department of Justice,
    Law Enforcement Assistance Administration,
    2nd ed., March, 1977.

    Excellent bibliography stressing recent
    materials. Detailed annotations. 168 entries,
    with index and publishers' addresses.

3. Boston, Guy D. <u>Terrorism: Supplement to the</u>
    <u>Second Edition: A Selected Bibliography</u>.
    Department of Justice, Law Enforcement
    Assistance Administration, September, 1977.

    An excellent bibliography of recent mater-
    ials. Most of the annotations are in excep-
    tional detail and prepared with great compe-
    tence. 83 entries.

4. Coxe, B. <u>Terrorism</u> (Bibliography). Air Force
    Academy, Colorado: Air Force Academy
    Library, 1977.

    Approximately 700 citations, most post-
    1969, are provided.

5. Felsenfeld, Lyn and Jenkins, Brian. <u>Interna-</u>
    <u>tional Terrorism: An Annotated Bibliogra-</u>
    <u>phy</u>. Santa Monica, Calif: Rand Corpora-
    tion, September, 1973.

6. Kelly, Michael J., and Mitchell, Thomas M.
   <u>Violence, Internal War and Revolution.</u>
   Ottawa: Norman Patterson School of International Affairs, Carlton University,
   April, 1976.

   Includes a special section on Canadian
   violence among its 496 citations, all of which
   have been carefully and intelligently chosen.

7. Keniston, K. <u>Radical Militants: An Annotated
   Bibliography of Empirical Research on Campus Unrest.</u> Lexington, Va.: Heath Lexington Books, 1973.

8. Khalidi, Walid, and Khadduri, Jill, eds. <u>Pa-
   lestine and the Arab-Israeli Conflict.</u>
   Beirut: Institute for Palestine Studies,
   and Kuwait: University of Kuwait, 1974.

   Over 4500 entries of which many deal with
   the Palestinian Resistance Movement (both pro
   and con). The bibliography is well organized
   and competently prepared.

9. Mannheim, J. B. and Wallace, M. <u>Political Violence in the United States, 1875-1974: A
   Bibliography.</u> New York: Garland Publishing, Inc., 1975.

10. Mikolus, Edward F. <u>Annotated Bibliography on
    Transnational and International Terrorism.</u>
    Washington: Central Intelligence Agency,
    1976.

    Over 1200 citations, most of which are an-
    notated. A very admirable research tool, al-
    though the user should carefully doublecheck
    the publication data.

11. Monroe, James L. <u>Prisoners of War and Politi-
    cal Hostages: A Select Bibliography.</u>
    Springfield, Va.: The Monroe Corporation
    for the U. S. Air Force, 1973.

    A 45 page bibliography.

12. Overholt, William H. <u>Revolution: A Biblio-
    graphy.</u> Croton-on-Hudson, N.Y.: Hudson
    Institute, January 9, 1975.

13. Piasetzki, J Peter. Urban Guerrilla Warfare and Terrorism: A Selected Bibliography. Monticello, Illinois: Council of Planning Librarians, 1976.

    16 pp. Concentrates on U.S. and Canadian versions of terrorism and political violence.

14. Russell, Charles A., et. al. "The Urban Guerrilla in Latin America: A Select Bibliography." Latin American Research Review. 9 (Spring, 1974): 37-79. (unseen)

15. U. N. Secretariat. International Terrorism: A Select Bibliography. New York: United Nations, September 26, 1973.

16. U. S. Department of Justice. Terrorist Activities: Bibliography. Quantico, Va.: FBI Academy, 1975.

    A 79 page bibliography which is especially useful for its coverage of law enforcement-oriented periodical articles.

17. _____. Hostage Situations: Bibliography. Quantico, Va.: FBI Academy, 1973.

    Includes about 100 references to hostage situations, airplane hijackings, bank robbery hostages, and preventive measures.

18. _____. Hostage Situations. Quantico, Va.: FBI Academy, January, 1975.

    Over 400 entries in this updated bibliography.

19. _____. Law Enforcement Assistance Administration. National Institute of Law Enforcement and Criminal Justice. Terrorism (Bibliography). Rockville, Md., 1978.

    A very intensive annotated bibliography (531 entries) including sources in English, French, Dutch, German, Italian, Serbo-Croatian, Spanish, et. al.

Appendix 1

In addition to the many sources which are provided in the body of the bibliography, the reader may wish to consult the following references:

Adelphi Papers (International Institute for Strategic Studies)
Air University Review
American Journal of International Law
Assets Protection
Chitty's Law Journal (Canada)
Comparative Strategy
Conflict
Counterforce
Department of State Bulletin
Dissent
Facts on File
FBI Law Enforcement Journal
Foreign Affairs
International Legal Materials
Journal of Palestine Studies
Middle East Journal
Military Police Law Enforcement Journal
Military Review
Naval War College Review
Parameters
Police Chief
Police Journal (England)
Survival
Terrorism

The reader should not only consult the standard periodical indexes (e.g. Public Affairs Information Service, Reader's Guide, etc.) but also the Air University Index to Military Periodicals, an indispensible and unique index, which is published quarterly and cumulated yearly.

202

Public Documents: The Congressional Record can be
a useful source for both public documents and published materials. Relatively obscure, but useful
materials are frequently submitted for the record,
thus making the Congressional Record a useful resource. In addition the National Criminal Justice
Reference Service (NCJRS), operated by the Law
Enforcement Assistance Administration (Box 6000,
Rockville, Md. 20850) will provide microfilm copies
of selected documents gratis. The NCJRS also op-
erates an interlibrary loan service.

Reports of congressional hearings can be especially
fertile as well, both for the record of expert tes-
timony and the appended documents which customarily
accompany such reports. The Index to Government
Publications should be consulted for such materials,
as well as other government publications dealing
with terrorism and allied subject matter.

Annual publications of note:

>   Annual of Power and Conflict
>   Canadian Yearbook of International Law
>   Digest of United States Practice in Inter-
>   national Law

Appendix 2

A. Twelve Essential Titles:

   1. Alexander and Finger, eds. <u>Terrorism: In-</u>
      <u>terdisciplinary Perspectives</u> (A4).

   2. Arendt. <u>On Violence</u> (C3).

   3. Bassiouni, ed. <u>International Terrorism and</u>
      <u>Political Crimes</u> (A12).

   4. Friedlander, ed. <u>Terrorism: Documents of</u>
      <u>International and Local Control</u> (A59).

   5. Laqueur. <u>Terrorism</u> (A111).

   6. Norton and Greenberg, eds. <u>Studies in Nu-</u>
      <u>clear Terrorism</u>. (M69)

   7. Rapoport, D. <u>Assassination and Terrorism</u>
      (A161).

   8. Sobel. <u>Political Terrorism</u>. (2 vols.)
      (A183, 184)

   9. U.S. Dept. of Justice. <u>Disorders and Ter-</u>
      <u>rorism</u> (A220).

   10. Walter. <u>Terror and Resistance</u> (V8).

   11. Wilkinson. <u>Political Terrorism</u> (A232).

   12. Wilkinson. <u>Terrorism and the Liberal State</u>
       (A231).

B. An Expanded Acquisitions List:

1. Alexander. <u>International Terrorism</u> (A2).

2. Avrich. <u>The Russian Anarchists</u> (D1).

3. Becker. <u>Hitler's Children</u> (O3).

4. Bell. <u>Terror Out of Zion</u> (M14).

5. Cooley. <u>Green March, Black September</u> (M27).

6. Crozier, ed. <u>Annual of Power and Conflict</u> (A44).

7. Curtis, et. al, eds. <u>The Palestinians</u> (M28).

8. Fanon. <u>The Wretched of the Earth</u> (C13).

9. Halperin. <u>Terrorism in Latin America</u> (L29).

10. Jenkins. International Terrorism: A New Mode of Conflict (A89).

11. Livingston. <u>International Terrorism in the Contemporary World</u> (A117).

12. Moss. <u>The War for the Cities</u> (A138).

13. Ochberg, ed. <u>Victims of Terrorism</u> (G(k)27).

14. Quandt, Jabber and Lesch. <u>Politics of Palestinian Nationalism</u> (M97).

15. U.S. Congress. <u>An Act to Combat International Terrorism</u> (A202, 203).

16. Woodcock. <u>Anarchism</u> (D19).

Index

Note: Section G (Tactics) is subdivided and coded as follows: (A) Assassination; (B) Bombings; (K) Kidnapping and Hostages; and (S) Skyjacking. (Add.) is used to denote Addendum in various chapters.

208

Hoffenberg, Jack U55
Hoffer, Eric C22
Hoffman, J. E. O30
Hoffman, Robert D9
Holden, David M51
Holt, Simma N15
Honerich, Ted C23
Hook, Sidney C24
Horchem, Hans J. O34, O35,
  O36
Horlick, Gary N. G(S)30
Horowitz, Irving Louis A74,
  A75, A76, A77, A78, D10,
  D11, L31
Horrell, Muriel J8
Horvitz, J. F. M52
Hosmer, Stephen T. K5
Household, Geoffrey U56,
  U57
Hoveyda, F. I6
Howard, A. J. O37
Howley, Dennis C. M53
Hubbard, David G(S)31
Huberman, Leo C25, L32
Hudson, Michael C. B63,
  M54, M55, M56
Huntington, Samuel B30
Hurewitz, Jacob C. M57
Hurwood, Bernhardt J.
  G(A)11
Hussain, Mehmood M58
Hutchinson, Martha
  Crenshaw A79, A80, H41,
  M59
Hyams, Edward A81, G(A)12

Ikle, Fred C. G(B)4
Imai, Ryukichi H42
Ingram, Timothy H. H43
Institute for the Study
  of Conflict M60, H44,
  P3, Q4
International Institute
  for Strategic Studies
  A82
IRA O38
Israel M61, M62
Israel Ministry for
  Foreign Affair G(S)32

Jabber, Fuad M63, M97
Jackson, Sir Geoffrey
  L33
Jacobs, Harold N16
Jacobs, W. D. J9
James, Daniel L34
Janke, Peter L35, O39
Jaquett, S. J. L36
Javits, Jacob K. A83
Jay, Martin N17
Jefferson, R. M. H78
Jenkins, Brian M. A84,
  A85, A86, A87, A88,
  A89, A90, A91, A92,
  A93, A94, A95, A96,
  A97, A98, A99, A229,
  G(K)14, G(K)15, G(K)16,
  H21, H45, H46, H47,
  R25, W5
Jenkins, Roy O40
Jepson, Selwyn U58
Johnpoll, Bernard N18,
  N19
Johnson, Chalmers A100,
  A101, A102, B31, B32
Johnson, Francis G(A)13
Johnson, Janera A85,
  G(K)14
Johnson, Kenneth F. L37,
  L38
Johnson, Kenneth L. L39
Joiner, Charles M64
Joll, James D12
Journal of Air, Law and
  Commerce G(S)33
Joyner, Nancy Douglas
  G(S)34

Kadi, Leila S. M65
Kahane, Meir N20
Kahn, E. J. Jr. A103
Kalb, Marvin U59
Kane, Henry U60
Kaplan, John G(A)14
Karber, Phillip A. A104,
  H48
Katz, Doris M66
Katz, Robert U61
Katz, Samuel M67

Morris, Michael J11, J12
Morris, Robert N26
Morris, Roger A228
Mort, Gustave N24
Mosbey, J. C. N27
Moss, Robert A136, A137,
  A138, A139, L47, O49
Mosse, Hilde L. A140
Most, Johann D14, D15
Moughrabi, Fouad M81
Mullen, Robert K. H63
Murphy, James G(K)24
Murphy, John F. F12, F39,
  G(K)25, I7
Murphy, Warren U84
Muslih, Muhammad Y. M82

Nachayev, Sergei D3
Nader, Ralph H64
Nahas, Dania M100
Naipaul, V. S. U72
Najmuddin, Dilshad G(K)26
Nakleh, Emile A. M83
Nasution, Abdul Haris A141
Neale, William D. A142
Neber, Tom Q5
Nesvold, B. B18
Nieburg, M. L. B47
Niezing, J. A143
Nkrumah, Kwave C40
Norden, Eric M84
Norman, Lloyd H65
Norton, Augustus R. H66,
  H67, H68, H69, H70,
  M85, M86, T7
Nuclear Energy, Policy
  Study Group H71
Nunez, Carlos L48

O'Ballance, Edgar K10,
  K11, M87, M88
O'Brien, Conor Cruise
  A144, A145
O'Brien, Kevin W2
O'Brien, Leon N28
Ochberg, Frank G(K)27
  G(K)28
O'Flaherty, Liam O50
O'Hearn, D. J. A134

O'Neill, Bard A146, M89,
  M90, M91
O'Neill, Edward A. U73
Oppenheimer, Martin A147
Oren, Uri G(S)42
Osanka, Franklin M. B48
Osmond, Andrew U74
Otis, David G(S)29
Overholt, William H. W12

Pace, Eric U75
Padover, Saul K. G(A)23
Paine, Lauran A148,
  G(A)24
Palestine Liberation
  Organization M92
Palmer, Bruce F40
Palumbo, Joanne W2
Paris, Edmund P4
Parker, Guy J. B49
Parker, Robert B. U76
Parry, Albert A149
Paul, Leslie A150
Paust, Jordan J. A151,
  A152, F41, F42, F43,
  F44, M93
Paxman, J. M. F34
Payne, Robert A153, A154
Payne, Ronald A47, A48
Pearsall, R. B. N29
Pendley, Robert H72
Pepitone, Albert B50
Pepper, Curtis B. G(K)29,
  O51, O52
Peretz, Don M94
Peterson, Edward A.
  G(S)43
Peterson, R. W. A155
Pfaff, William A157
Phillips, David G(S)44,
  G(S)52
Piasetzki, J. Peter W13
Pierre, Andrew J. A156
Pike, Douglas K12,
  K(Add.)
Pike, Earl A. G(B)7
Pincus, Walter H73
Pitts, Denis U77
Plastrik, S. A158
Platero. D. G(K)30

214

Seaman, Donald U85
Sears, D. D. N38
Security Gazette S11
Sederberg, Peter C. V6
Segre, D. V. A171
Sela, Owen U86
Sewell, Alan F. A172
Seymour, Gerald U87, U88
Shapley, Deborah H84
Sharabi, Misham M104, M105
Shatz, Marshall S. D17
Shaw, P. D. S12
Shearer, I. A. F51
Sheehan, Edward R. F. M106
Shepard, Ira M. F52
Shipley, P. A173
Short, J. F. B55
Shriver, R. B., Jr. S13
Shudder, Sami G(S)49
Shulman, Alix K. B56
Shultz, Richard A174
Silj, Alessandro O(Add.)
Silverstein, Martin E.
  S14, S15
Sim, Richard A175
Simon, Douglas W. G(K)31
Simp, Howard R. A(Add.)
Sinclair, Andrew E10, L52
Singer, L. W. S16
Singh, Baljit A176, B57
Singh, Khushwant K16
Singh, Satindra K16
Skeptic, The A177
Skobnick, Jerome B58
Slater, Leonard M107
Sliwowski, George F53
Sloan, Stephen A178, A179,
  R22
Smart, Ian M. H. A180
Smernoff, Barry J. H26
Smith, Clifford V. H85
Smith, Colin A181
Smith, Corin L. G(S)50
Smith, D. A182
Smith, McKeithen R. N.
  G(S)51
Smith, R. D. R23
Smith, Roger H86
Snow, Peter G(S)52
Sobel, Lester A. A183,
  A184, M108

Solinas, Franco L12
Solzhenitsyn, Alexander
  V7
Sorel, Georges C42
Souchon, Henri G(K)32
South African Institute
  of Race Relations J13,
  J14
Soviet Union M109
Sparrow, Gerald G(A)26
Spjut, R. J. T8
Sponsler, T. H. G(K)33
Stafford, David O57
Stanley Foundation, The
  H88
Stechel, Ira G(K)34
Steelman, H. G(S)53
Steinhilper, G. R24
Steinhoff, Patricia K17
Sterling, Claire A185
Stern, Susan E11
Stetler, Russell M110
Stevenson, Adlai E. III
  H87
Stevenson, William G(S)54
Stewart, James N39
Stiles, Dennis W. A186
Stirner, Max D18
Stoffel, John G(B)8
Stohl, Michael A187
Stolz, Matthew F. B59
Storr, Anthony A188
Stratton, J. G. G(K)35
  G(K)36
Street, M. O58
Strentz, Thomas A189,
  G(K)37
Strickler, Nina C43
Stules, S. G. G(B)9
Suarez, Hector Victor L53
Suchlicki, Jaime B60
Sullivan, Gerald R25
Sundberg, M. Jacob F54,
  O59
Sundiata, I. K. J15
Sweezy, Paul M. C25, L32
Synge, T. M. F55
Syrkin, Marie A190

Taber, Robert B61

216

DATE DUE